HOW TO BUILD YOUR DREAM HOME!

A Place for Couples, Kids & Comfort

by Steve Klein & Jeff May

How To Build Your Dream Home!
A Place for Couples, Kids & Comfort
Copyright © 2017 Steve Klein & Jeff May

ISBN 978-1548692414

DEDICATION

In honor of our parents and the parents of our wives:

Clayton and Kathleen Klein

James and Glenda May

Carrol and Mamie Sutton

Billy and Ruth Henderson

ACKNOWLEDGMENTS

Proofreading:
Shirley Holt
Katie Klein

CONTENTS

Preface

This book is written primarily for Christians who are married or who are contemplating marriage. It may be used profitably by husbands and wives individually or together, by small groups in home studies, or by church-arranged Bible classes. For the latter, we recommend planning to take two class periods to cover each lesson.

The material in this volume has been used by the authors for many years to counsel couples, preach sermons, and teach Bible classes. Along the way, we have learned from other students of God's plan for the home, but we cannot always recall the source of a concept or idea. Nonetheless, to the best of our recollection, we have diligently attempted to give appropriate credit to known sources throughout this book.

The authors strongly believe that God's word, the Bible, contains the ideal plan for the home. God designed us, and He designed the home for us. If each family member will commit to knowing and following God's plan, the home can become a wondrous place for nurturing human souls who are being prepared in this life for their eternal home with God. While neither author claims to have the perfect home, we have both found that when God's plan is applied by everyone in the family, it works wonderfully well.

May the Lord richly bless your study,
Steve Klein & Jeff May

1

Chapter 1

God Wants Your Home to be Beautiful

THE INTENT OF THIS STUDY

Some time ago, a married couple envisioned the building of their "dream house." They planned a large country home (several thousand square feet with a full basement) in a secluded area of Limestone County, Alabama. Building began and seemed to be progressing well. The basement was dug. Then, abruptly, the building stopped. Why? The couple was experiencing marital problems. Lawyers must have been called in and papers filed, because before long the divorce was final. Now a basement without a house above it sits as a monument to failed dreams and to the foolishness of planning to build one kind of home while neglecting another.

A *house* is a dwelling—a physical structure designed to shelter humans. Everyone must have a place to dwell. But the word *home* can convey so much more. It suggests a relationship between people. As Webster's dictionary puts it, the home is *"the social unit formed by a family living together."*

Obviously, the focus of this study is not how to build physical structures for family dwellings, but how to build the family itself. God is the great Architect of the home, and we must build it according to His specifications if we expect it to stand as a refuge in life's storms (Matthew 7:24-27).

God designed the home to be an extraordinary blessing to every man and woman He joins together in marriage. Notice the recurring theme of *joy* and *happiness* in the following Scriptures:

Let your fountain be blessed,
And rejoice with the wife of your youth.
(Proverbs 5:18)

He who finds a wife finds a good thing,
And obtains favor from the Lord.
(Proverbs 18:22)

Live joyfully with the wife whom you love
all the days of your vain life which He has
given you under the sun.
(Ecclesiastes 9:9)

When a man has taken a new wife, he shall not go out to
war or be charged with any business; he shall be
free at home one year, and bring happiness to
his wife whom he has taken.
(Deuteronomy 24:5)

As we will discover in the course of our study, the blessings God wants to come from marriage are numberless. They include...

- **Companionship and help** (Gen. 2:18-25). See Adam's excitement!!

- **Fulfillment and happiness**

- **A nest** – a safe and comfortable place to settle into and rest.

- **An appreciation for the love of family.** An understanding of *family love* is critical to many human relationships, especially within the spiritual family of God. Consider that God calls our union with His Son a marriage. He is a Father. We are sons and daughters, and we have brothers and sisters, all of whom we are to love in a familial way (Heb. 13:1)!

- **The development of strong and righteous nations** (Prov. 14:34).

- **A place to learn to be a servant.** To become Christlike and fulfill God's eternal purpose for you, you must learn to become a servant. It's not about you! The home is the perfect place to learn what loving service is all about.

Yet, with all these blessings (and many more) that can be received in a godly home, some may still wonder, *"**Why should I study what the Bible says about the home?**"* Here are the reasons:

HOMES ARE UNDER ATTACK

In the 1962 book, *Marriage is for Those Who Love God and One Another,* author Thomas Warren noted the frontal attack then being made on the family in some nations by Communist and Marxist philosophies. Then he makes the following statement: *"In our own great nation, there is no deliberate, ideological, or concerted attack on marriage and the family...."* To those of us living in the new millennium, it seems incredible that such a statement could have been made just a few decades ago.

Today the home is being attacked on every side. Groups advancing homosexual rights and feminism are especially vigorous in their efforts to destroy the family structure as Christians have known it and as God ordained it. The recent legalization of homosexual marriage in the United States is just one result of an ongoing cultural assault on Biblical values. There is never a stalemate in the struggle between good and evil (cf. Eph. 5:11ff.). We cannot stand by and *do nothing* and expect ourselves and our children to enjoy godly homes.

HOME IS THE CENTER OF LIFE

Tavek is a Hebrew word which usually refers to the middle or center of something. Genesis 3:3 states that the tree of life grew in the "midst *(tavek)* of the garden." Deuteronomy 21:12 instructs the men of Israel about what to do with a new wife taken from captives – "bring her home *(tavek)* to your house (Heb. *bayith*)." There seems to be an implication here that the home is "the center" of a human being's life. It is the hub of our daily activities! The daily activities that occurred in the homes of Bible characters occur in our homes as well:

- Eating (Acts 2:46; 1 Corinthians 11:34)
- Sleeping (Luke 11:7; Job 33:15)
- Loving and being loved (Titus 2:4)
- Learning (Ephesians 6:4; 1 Corinthians 14:35)
- Meditating (Psalm 63:6)
- Praying (Acts 10:30)

When things are not right at home, our entire lives are *off-center!*

HOMES ARE FAILING

Probably none of us needs to be told that homes are crumbling in our culture. But in case you need any verification of your suspicions along this line, note these grim statistics:

- In 1960, 5.3% of births were to unmarried women. By 2012 that number had risen to 40.7% of all children born in the United States.[1] Nearly half of these receive food stamps or welfare.

- In 1960, there were 292 recorded abortions in the United States. Every year since 1975, there have been over one

---

[1] U.S. Census Bureau, 2013

million abortions in America.[2]

- In the 1860's, the divorce rate in America was 3%. By 1960, the number of divorces was equal to about 25% of the number of marriages that year. By 2011, divorces had risen to more than 50% of the number of marriages.

- In 1960, 463,000 children were directly affected by divorce.[3] That number has more than doubled. It is estimated that half of all American children will witness the breakup of their parents' marriage.

These sad statistics illustrate that homes not built according to God's plans will not stand. *"Unless the Lord builds the house, they labor in vain who build it..."* (Psalm 127:1). If we want a dream home that lasts, we must know and follow God's plans.

SOME CHRISTIANS ARE DISENCHANTED WITH THE DREAM

"The Home" is a sermon topic often requested by church members. In fact, many preachers would tell you that it is *the most frequently requested* sermon topic. These requests reflect a desire for homes that are happy and blessed, but may also imply that many Christians are dissatisfied with their own home lives. Their knowledge of what *should be* in comparison to what *actually is* only serves to make them unhappy.

Most of the problems for which people ask Biblical counseling and advice relate to relationships in the home. Typically, one family member is unhappy because another family member is not behaving as a Christian should in the home. But with very little probing, the discovery is often made that the family member asking for help is also not doing what God would have him or her do.

---

[2] Historical abortion statistics, United States compiled by Wm. Robert Johnston
[3] Statistics from the *American Family Association Journal, January, 1995.*

Without judging motives, it appears that some folks are not wanting preaching and teaching on the home for the purpose of self-improvement, but so that they might selfishly "get their way" in their home lives. As those who went to hear Ezekiel preach, *"with their mouth they show much love, but their hearts pursue their own gain"* (Ezek. 33:31).

Happiness in the home is desired but often not possessed, because even when God's plan is known, it is not followed. It will not be enough simply to acquaint ourselves with God's design. Once we know God's plan, we must do what we know. Each of us must determine to actually build according to His design! This is the principle Jesus Himself was stressing in John 13:17 when He told His disciples, *"If you know these things, happy are you IF YOU DO THEM"* (emph. mine – SK).

OUR ETERNAL DESTINIES ARE AT STAKE

It is more than just *unfortunate* when homes are broken by divorce, or when they remain intact but are filled with misery, abuse, dissatisfaction, and loneliness. It is sin (1 John 3:4)! And sin is often a consequence of failing to know and understand God's will.

The lack of knowing God's will leads to destruction (Hosea 4:6). Those who do know God's design for the home need to be motivated to apply what they know; failing to do this is also sin (James 4:17)! When judgment comes, sins relative to home life will certainly send more than a few surprised souls to eternal punishment (2 Thess. 1:7-9). Please allow that sobering reality to grab your attention and stimulate you to give your most diligent effort to this study.

If you are married, God wants you to have a mountaintop marriage! He wants it not only because He wants you to be happy in this life, but so that you might one day live with Him in His eternal home. If you are not married, you need to know what God's expectations are. It will help improve your other family relationships with parents and siblings, it will help you to become a better Christian, and it will make you more prepared should the Lord bless your life with marriage in the future.

QUESTIONS

1. What is your definition of a *home* in the sense we are studying?

2. What is the relationship between a *house* and a *home*?

3. In Matthew 7:24-27, Jesus uses an illustration of housebuilding which, although meant to apply to every area of life, certainly applies to the building of a godly home. Study this text and answer the following:

    a. Will we be wise homebuilders if we just hear God's word? What else is required?

    b. What are some of the storms of life that a family may face?

4. What word does the Bible use to describe the action of a person who knows what God wants him to do but does not do it (James 4:17)?

5. List as many sins as you can think of (either of omission or commission) which are commonly committed in the home by each of the following:

    a. Husbands

    b. Wives

    c. Parents

    d. Children

6. What are some of the activities that go on in the home on a daily basis that make it the hub of daily life?

7. In your opinion, what single statistic most strongly indicates that the home is failing in our culture?

8. What must YOU do to have a happy home life?

9. What reasons are given in this lesson for studying the home?

10. Can you think of any additional reasons which would motivate you personally to study the home?

Chapter 2

The Design of the Home

GOD DESIGNED THE HOME

Somewhere in eternity past, God dreamed of the kind of home that would be best for us and bless our lives abundantly. He consulted with no one. As the One who stitched us together in the womb, He knew exactly what we needed to thrive in this life and prepare for the next. He needed no CAD system to assist Him in His drafting because His mind surpasses ours *"as far as the heavens are above the earth"* (Isa. 55:8-9). No human mind or motherboard can even come close.

Yet, it's amazing how we earthlings manage to deny that there is one supreme and unequaled blueprint for the home. We scratch out our drafts of homes with single parents, matriarchs, homosexual parents, or even temporary living arrangements. Pridefully, we then feel that we have sketched a design that will equal or even surpass His Master plan.

We must remember that God has only *one ideal* plan. It is His *"holy institution which He loves"* and must never be downsized, altered, or downright profaned (Mal. 2:11). God planned the home the way He wanted it, and His plan is the best.

His blueprint is not copyrighted! He intends for it to be copied and shared in every home. So follow it carefully and share it freely. It is the only one that provides for complete human happiness. Nothing else will work. As we noted in Chapter 1, *"Unless the Lord builds the house, they labor in vain who build it"* (Psalm 127:1).

Unfortunately, many homes are not ideal due to circumstances that could not be controlled (such as divorce due to a spouse's unfaithfulness or even a tragic death). With understanding and compassionate hearts, we pray for those homes. God can help what is lacking. Not having the ideal home is no reason to scrap God's plan entirely. To whatever degree it is possible, we should adhere to God's design for our lives!

GOD DESIGNED THE HOME AS A UNIT

A unit is something made up of component parts which fit together and complement one another so that they work **as one**. God made the home a unit.

In Matthew 19:4-6, when Jesus spoke of the marriage unit, He knew to go back to the original blueprint. He went back where the drawing was clear: the drawing board of God set in the beginning. He knew the old blueprint never fails and must not be replaced with another.

Genesis 2:18-24 concludes with these words: *"Therefore a man shall leave his father and mother and be joined to his wife, and they shall become **one flesh**."*

The word "one" in these passages identifies the home as a unit. No part in it exists for its own benefit but for the good of the whole. Each part must do its job in order for the unit to work properly.

GOD DESIGNED THE COMPONENT PARTS OF THE HOME

Can we see God in the beginning putting various parts together in the home? He made sure everything in it was needed and properly placed. He even made adjustments after allowing Adam to see that something was missing and desperately needed. He said, *"It is not good that a man should be alone; I will make him a helper comparable to him"* (Gen. 2:18).

God knew exactly what Adam needed, so He made another part for the home. He made that *"helper comparable to him,"* or as other translations say, a *"help meet for him"* (KJV), or *"a helper suitable for him"* (NIV, NASB).

Strong's Hebrew Dictionary defines the word translated "comparable" as the *"part opposite, specifically a counterpart or mate."* Woman is the "part opposite" man; she is made with expert precision to complete the human unit we call "home." When Adam saw her, you can hear the excitement in His voice. At last, His loving God had created someone to fit perfectly with him. He called her "woman," but someone has well said that it was like he saw her and said, "Woah-man!" Here was someone beautifully unlike him and amazingly like him at the same time—*"bone of my bones, and flesh of my flesh"* (Gen. 2:23). She's the half that makes him whole.

The fact that man and woman were *designed* from the beginning to be complimentary parts of a single unit is of far-reaching significance. It demands that men and women respect the uniqueness of their God-given roles and see the necessity of fulfilling them. It clearly defines the reason that polygamous and homosexual marriages are just wrong. Some parts were never created by God to be placed into a marriage. They are faulty, human designs.

To illustrate, an automobile has hundreds of component parts, but for sake of illustration let us view it as having only two main parts—the engine and the body. Each of these parts was designed for the other. Both parts must be united to have a functional automobile. Two bodies with one engine won't work. Two engines or two bodies together won't work. Even so, the home must be composed of one man and one woman functioning as God designed.

GOD DESIGNED THE HOME WITH "ROOMS"

In a house, rooms are designed to meet certain needs or desires. A person can go to bed in the "bedroom," dine in the "dining room," and bathe in the "bathroom" (it might even be possible to hibernate in the "den").

God's word declares that *"Through wisdom a house is built, and by understanding it is established; by knowledge **the rooms are filled with all precious and pleasant riches**"* (Prov. 24:3-4). This passage speaks of beautiful things that fill the rooms of a home. This is not an emphasis on the furnishings. It is about the beautiful things God has provided for you in the home. It is about being the right kind of marriage partner, parent, or child.

To amplify Proverbs 24:3-4, consider this question: If you turned on to the road that leads to your house later tonight and found your house burned down to the foundation, but your family was unscathed, what beautiful things about your home *would not* have been destroyed? Those are the things we are emphasizing in this study. Those are the things designed by the wisdom of God to fill the home.[4]

You see, God designed the home to meet human needs. Since He alone knows the intricacies of the human frame (Ps. 103:14; 139:15), the rooms He has planned for the home correspond exactly to the needs of man. God's *purpose* for the home is to provide for these needs. We will write in more detail on the various rooms of the home in lesson four, but for now, notice that this design includes…

(1) **Room for companionship.** From the beginning, God saw that *"it is not good that man should be alone"* (Gen. 2:18). Man needs company, and in response God creates woman and *"sets the solitary in families"* (Psalm 68:6).

---

[4] Adapted from Charles Swindoll, *Strike the Original Match*, (Grand Rapids, MI: Zondervan, 1993).

Therefore, *"he who finds a wife finds a good thing, and obtains favor from the Lord"* (Prov. 18:22, cf. Eccl. 9:9; Mal. 2:14b).

(2) Room for procreation. The survival of any species depends upon procreation. God's expressed will is that all His creatures *"be fruitful and multiply"* (Gen. 1:22). Among humans, God has designed the home as the place for procreation (Gen. 1:28; 9:1). He has made the family a unit because He seeks godly offspring (Mal. 2:15).

(3) Room for gratification. In conjunction with the need to procreate, God has given men and women a strong sexual desire. God created humans capable of gratifying their sexual desires virtually anytime after reaching biological maturity. This ability, meant as a blessing to humans, becomes a moral and biological curse when it is exercised without limits. But God has provided for the full and free gratification of human sexual desires within the home (Heb. 13:4).

Furthermore, a man is to drink water from his own cistern (his own wife), and so find complete and continual satisfaction for his sexual thirst (Prov. 5:15-19). As a preventative to fornication, both husband and wife are to relinquish control of their own bodies to each another, and are commanded not to *"deprive"* one another (1 Cor. 7:1-5).

(4) Room for societal order. In order for man to thrive in a society, the society must have order and stability. According to Gibbon, one of the main reasons for *The Decline and Fall of the Roman Empire* was "the rapid increase in divorce: the undermining of the dignity and sanctity of the home, which is the basis of human society."

In early Bible times, the family wasn't the *basis* for society—it *was* society. In that *Patriarchal Dispensation*, God dealt with people primarily through the heads of families. As the population grew, *society* often took the form of *tribes*, which were basically extended families. The connection between the family, the tribe, and the nation is clearly seen in Abraham.

As a Patriarch, the Lord had promised Abraham that he would be the *"father of many nations"* and become *"a great and mighty nation"* (Gen. 17:4-5; 18:18). The things Abraham's children were taught at home were to serve to anchor the nation. He was to *"command his children and his household after him, that they keep the way of the LORD, to do righteousness and justice, that the LORD may bring to Abraham what He has spoken to him"* (Gen. 18:19).

Homes are designed to provide humans with the training necessary for maintaining societal order. In homes we should learn respect for authority, honesty, hard work, teamwork, faithfulness, responsibility, accountability, and dedication. We love the words of former first lady Barbara Bush who said, "Your success as a family... our success as a nation... depends not on what happens inside the White House, but on what happens inside your house."

GOD DESIGNED THE HOME AS A PERMANENT STRUCTURE

The home designed by God is to last till death (Rom. 7:2). Divorce for just any reason is not lawful (Matt. 19:3-5). *"Therefore what God has joined together, let not man separate."* God *"hates divorce"* for *"it covers one's garment with violence"* (Mal. 2:16). Divorce does violence to the spouse and violence against the expressed will of God concerning marriage.

God allows for ONE exception to His no-divorce design. It is found in Matthew 19:9.

Please notice the following truths concerning this exception:

- The ONLY reason God will accept for divorce is sexual immorality on the part of one's spouse.

- The sexual immorality must be the "reason" for the divorce action (Matt. 5:32).

- The innocent spouse is to divorce or put away the guilty spouse. The word *divorce* as Jesus uses it is a transitive verb. It involves something one does *to* another.

- Adultery is committed any time a person who has *been unscripturally divorced* marries another.

False doctrines have arisen seeking to justify those who have divorced for any cause; these doctrines attempt to scrap God's design for the home. While a full examination of these doctrines is beyond the scope of this study, we hope the following comments directed at three of **these false doctrines** will be especially helpful.

(1) God's marriage law does apply to the non-Christian.
God designed marriage for the whole human race. The design revealed in Genesis 1 and Matthew 19 was revealed to non-Christians. If those outside of Christ are not subject to God's laws for marriage, it would be impossible for them to sin by violating a marriage law (1 John 3:4; Rom. 2:12). But we know from Scripture that there are those outside of Christ who are fornicators and adulterers (1 Cor. 5:9-11; 6:9-11).

(2) Divorce is not granted for desertion. In 1 Corinthians 7:13-15, Paul allows that the Christian whose unbelieving spouse will not dwell with them is "not under bondage in such cases." The *bondage* under consideration is the duties of spousal service. The deserted spouse is not obligated to chase their spouse all over the country trying to be a husband or wife to them. The Greek word used here for bondage (*douloo*) refers to service offered by obligation, such as that of a slave or bond servant. *It is never used to refer to the marriage bond.* Another Greek word (*deo*) is used when the marriage bond is in view (cf. 1 Cor. 7:27, 39; Rom. 7:2).

(3) Baptism does not wash away marriages. Baptism washes away sins (Acts 22:16) *if* one has repented of the sins (Acts 2:38). Could a polygamist continue to live with several wives after being baptized? Could a homosexual live with his same-sex spouse? Doesn't repentance demand that the unlawful situations created by sin be corrected (cf. Ezra 10:10-12)?

Building a marriage is like building a new house according to God's blueprint. When we first start to build, it's exciting. Everything is new and has a lot of luster to it. But if we are not careful, the emotions can be allowed to subside, the luster can wear off, and our excitement about each other can dwindle. Someone has said that a **"honeymoon is that time between bells and bills."**

Eventually, in every home, bills become due, weeds sprout, doors squeak and sag, windows stick, paint peels, a roof might leak, faucets drip, drains clog, floors get "dinged," and things get old. With a house, we've got three choices: *abandon the home, ignore the problems,* or *get to work.* With marriage, God doesn't want us to walk out or ignore the problems. He wants our homes to be structurally-sound, beautifully-furnished habitations. **He wants us to work at fixing whatever needs to be fixed.** We can do it!![5]

The most important thing you can allow to happen in a marriage is for **YOU** to let yourself be remodeled by God. The question is not: *"How do I want to design my home to make me happy?"* The question is: *"How did God design the home so that I can be TRULY happy?* (2 Cor. 5:15). If you do that, you are headed in the direction of a mountaintop marriage!!

---

[5] Swindoll, *Strike the Original Match.*

QUESTIONS

1. Why is it important for us to always remember that marriage originated with God?

2. Why is God best qualified to design the home?

3. Why isn't one design for the home just as good as another? Why will human designs for the home never be as good as God's design?

4. What happens in a home where God's will for the marriage is not considered? Do you observe the marriages being long-lasting, solid and fulfilling?

5. What were God's purposes in designing the home?

6. So many problems could be stopped if we simply slowed down to ask ourselves, "Am I behaving at this moment like God wants me to in my marriage?" We often do damaging things without even stopping to think. Give some examples of this.

7. What human needs has God made a room in the home to fulfill?

8. Explain how the home brings order to society.

9. Is it lawful for a man to divorce his wife for just any reason?

   Is it lawful for a man to divorce his wife for any reason other than fornication?

10. Why do you think God designed the home to be as permanent as life?

11. How do we know that God's marriage laws apply to those who are not Christians?

12. Would baptism *alone* be enough to receive forgiveness if one had married unlawfully in the past? Why or why not?

13. What does God want us to do with our home lives when they lose their luster or develop problems?

14. What's the most important thing you can do in a marriage, or in any relationship, to improve it?

Chapter 3

Laying a Solid Foundation

In February of 2013 in Seffner, Florida, a twenty-foot sinkhole formed under Jeff Bush's bedroom as he turned in for the night. As the floor vanished from under him, he screamed out for help. His brother Jeremy ran to the bedroom and witnessed a literal nightmare. Bush and all his furnishings had vanished into the earth. His remains never were recovered. What a tragedy!

In the next few months residents living throughout that region lived in fear that the same could happen to them. One man I am aware of said, "I have developed anxiety and can't sleep at night." Such is very understandable. We don't want to be gobbled up by the earth. We want stable foundations. We become very concerned when we see cracks in the house—especially if they're big ones! It's a sure sign that there is a problem at the foundation.

But what if the spiritual foundation of our home is not secure? More than physical life is at stake. Souls are in danger. Everything depends on the foundation. Jesus made sure He told us about that in His phenomenal Sermon on the Mount (cf. Matt. 7:23-27). Are you seeing any cracks? If so, you better consult the Lord, the Supreme Foundation Specialist.

CHRIST IS THE FOUNDATION AND CHIEF CORNERSTONE

Jesus Christ is the foundation and chief cornerstone of our relationships with God and each other in His church (Eph. 2:19-20; 1 Cor. 3:10-11). Oh, we can have relationships that are not built upon Christ with family, friends, coworkers and even the government, but they will always be mundane as though something is missing. But when we become Christians, everything changes in a most wonderful way.

Anytime Jesus touched anything or anyone during His life, things were always better. You could count on it. The Christian is a new creature, and all his relationships have a newfound aliveness to them because Christ is brought into all of them (2 Cor. 5:16-17). Every good thing is now done for *"the Lord's sake"* and *"as unto the Lord"* (1 Pet. 2:13; Col. 3:23).

If this is true when it comes to the relationships with government (Rom. 13:1-6) and employers (Col. 3:22-25; 4:1; 2 Thess. 3:10-12), it is vitally true when it comes to relationships within the home. Our relationship with Christ affects relationships in the home.

Notice Paul's instructions concerning the duties of young wives in Titus 2:4-5. They need to *"love their husbands, to love their children...that the word of God may not be blasphemed!"* Similarly, husbands must dwell with their wives *"with understanding...that your prayers may not be hindered!"* (1 Peter 3:7). And, if anyone does not provide for his own family, *"he has denied the faith"* (1 Tim. 5:8). Do you see it? All of these passages are implying that proper dealings with one another in the home are plumb-lined to our relationship with Jesus Christ.

For Christians, THE KEY to beginning to build an ideal home is realizing that every relationship must be governed by Jesus Christ. The Lord cannot be just a piece of our pie; He is the sweetness that permeates the whole pie! No part of our lives is marked *off-limits* to Him. We are foolish if we post such signs and refuse to allow Him on our property.

Four main pillars must then be set on this foundation, upon which the remainder of the home will rest.

PILLAR #1 – COMMITMENT

God designed marriage with the intent that a man would *"leave his father and mother and be joined to his wife"* (Gen. 2:24; cf. Eph. 5:31; Matt. 19:5). The Hebrew and Greek words translated "joined" in these passages mean "to adhere" or "to glue to." This indicates that the husband is to be committed to permanent union with his wife. For both the husband and wife, this commitment *necessitates* that two other options be permanently closed.

(1) There can be no thought of going back home to father and mother – you've got to *leave.* When asked to name the biggest cause of divorce, one judge is said to have quipped, *"In-laws!"* While honor and respect are due parents throughout life (cf. 1 Tim. 5:4; Prov. 31:28), no married person has a right to have parental ties which rival or disrupt the union to his or her spouse. Simply put, cut the umbilical cord! Leave and cleave.

(2) There can be no thought of what it would be like to *join* with another. The choice of a spouse automatically eliminates every other alternative. In his book, *The Art of Living,* Andre Maurois has suggested that this vow be made part of every marriage ceremony: *"I bind myself for life! I have chosen; from now on my aim will be, not to search for someone who may please me, but to please the one I have chosen."* To this Maurois adds, *"This decision can alone produce a successful marriage."* On the other hand, entering marriage with the thought that *"if it doesn't work out, I can always get a divorce and find someone else"* virtually guarantees that the home will be unstable. There's a huge crack revealed by even thinking such a thought.

PILLAR #2 – TRUST

Samson illustrates the problems a lack of trust causes in a marriage. His first love was a woman from Timnah—a daughter of the Philistines (Judges 14:1). At their wedding feast, Samson posed a riddle to his Philistine guests which none could initially answer (Judges 14:12-14). But when they pressured Samson's new wife, she enticed Samson to explain the riddle to her. Then she immediately went and told it to *"the sons of her people."* The marriage was over before it began. Samson left the feast in a rage, and his wife was given to his best man (Judges 14:15-20).

Considering Samson's initial experience with homebuilding, it is no wonder that his later relationships with women were sordid, unfulfilling and fraught with mistrust. Without trust, a marriage relationship cannot support itself. It is a challenging thing to give yourself wholly in union to another person. If you cannot trust that person, you will always be tempted to withhold part of yourself from them.

Of the virtuous wife Proverbs 31:11-12 states that *"the heart of her husband **safely trusts her**...she does him good and not evil all the days of her life."* Many aspects of home life require that spouses be able to *"safely trust"* one another. In each of their spheres of responsibility, husbands and wives must manage money, discipline children, handle sensitive personal information, and endure times of separation. Just planning the activities of the day will often require confidence that spouses are going to do what they say they will do, be where they say they will be, and be there when they say they will be there. Each must *trust* AND be *trustworthy.*

PILLAR #3 – RESPECT

God instructs the husband to give *"honor to the wife as to the weaker vessel"* (1 Peter 3:7). The word "honor" means to value or to esteem in the highest degree. She is like the fine china that is displayed proudly yet handled very carefully. Why? She's valuable. In similar fashion, the wife is told to *"see that she respects her husband"* (Eph. 5:33). Wives are to have the same attitude Sarah exhibited in calling her husband "lord" (1 Peter 3:6). He is treated like the king of the castle. And then children are told to *"honor your father and your mother"* (Eph. 6:2).

Mutual respect is a foundational pillar of every good home. Husbands and wives, and eventually parents and children, *must* possess a high positive regard for one another. So much that goes on in the home depends on it. Will a wife submit to a husband she does not respect? Will children obey parents they do not respect? Will a husband allow his wife the freedom to "manage the house" if he does not respect her?

Mutual respect between family members means that each will *highly value* the other's work, opinions, thoughts, words, approval, and love. In a home where people act as they should and communicate well with one another, it soon becomes obvious that home is undergirded with the pillar of respect.

In later chapters, we will look more closely at the responsibilities of husbands, wives, and children. We will once again see how crucial the pillar of respect really is.

PILLAR #4 – LOVE

There is a wide range of meaning in our English word *love.* We use the same word to express our feelings toward our car that we use to express our feelings toward our Creator. The term "love" can express everything from an appreciation for physical qualities to the selfless whole-hearted devotion of one who gives his life for his friends (cf. John 15:13). Within this range of meaning, three kinds of love are important in a marriage. To the ancient Greeks, *eros* was sexual love, *philos* was friendship love, and *agape* was a spiritual love which manifested itself in self-sacrificing devotion. Each of these kinds of love is vital to a marriage, and the third kind *(agape)* is a strong pillar in the foundation of a home.

- **Romantic and sexual love.** A desire to become and remain *lovers* is at the foundation of many homes. *"Where does a family start?"* asked Winston Churchill. *"It starts,"* he said, *"with a man falling in love with a girl; no superior alternative has yet been found."*

  The Song of Solomon details for us the place of "falling in love." There we learn that God celebrates romance and sex in a husband and wife relationship. It was all His idea in the first place. It may be God who speaks to these lovers in 5:1 saying, *"Eat O friends! Drink, yes, drink deeply, O beloved ones!"* Sexual relations in marriage are often compared to the drinking from a bountiful feast (Prov. 5:15-19). Because they belong to each other and desire to always freely give themselves to one another, they lack no passion in building a home that protects and nourishes their love for a lifetime.

  The bride of the Song begs, *"Let him kiss me with the kisses of his mouth, for your love is better than wine"* (Song of Sol. 1:2). "The Hebrew word translated 'love' here is **dodem**, which often refers to sexual love" (Dillow, *Solomon on Sex*). Albert Barnes comments that this refers to "endearments or tokens of affection." Its usages in Proverbs 7:18 and Ezekiel 23:17 clearly show how it is used in Scripture to refer to sexual love. This same basic word (Heb. *"dod"*) is translated "beloved" thirty-seven times in the Song of Solomon. From the outset and throughout married life, husbands and wives are to be "lovers."

- **Affectionate, feeling, friendship love.** The husband and wife in the Song of Solomon viewed themselves as friends. The husband did not view the wife as a mere sex object or a piece of property; he had warm feelings for her, as he would a sister. Four times he refers to her as *"my sister, my spouse"* (Song of Sol. 4:9, 10, 12; 5:1). Similarly the wife viewed the husband, not just as a lover, but a friend.

She says, *"His mouth is most sweet. Yes, he is altogether lovely. This is my beloved, and this is my friend..."* (Song of Sol. 5:16). Feelings of warmth and friendship which stem from shared time, interests, and purposes are also a key to a well-built home.

- **Sacrificial love.** *Agape* love is love which is concerned first and foremost with what is best for the person you love. This is the kind of love God had for man in sending His Son to die for us (John 3:16). This kind of love is commanded of husbands toward their wives (Eph. 5:25ff.). This kind of love leads family members to behave in specific ways which ensure the structural integrity of the home. In 1 Corinthians 13:4-8a, the actions of *agape* love are described:

> *Love suffers long and is kind;*
> *love does not envy;*
> *love does not parade itself, is not puffed up;*
> *does not behave rudely,*
> *does not seek its own,*
> *is not provoked,*
> *thinks no evil;*
> *does not rejoice in iniquity, but rejoices in the truth;*
> *bears all things,*
> *believes all things,*
> *hopes all things,*
> *endures all things.*
> *Love never fails..."*

With the force of this inspired description of love fully in our minds, it is easy to see that when the power of *agape* love governs the lives of every family member, homes will stand and flourish as God designed them to do. Remember, there are no hidden sinkholes in the God-built home.

QUESTIONS

1. Do you agree that "Christ becomes the foundation and chief cornerstone of every relationship the new Christian has"?

   - If this is true, how would it change the new Christian's relationship with government?

   - With employers?

   - In the home?

2. Which Bible passages would you use to show that our dealings with one another in the home have a direct connection to our relationship to Jesus Christ?

3. Further define the word "join" as it occurs in Genesis 2:24, Ephesians 5:31, and Matthew 19:5.

4. What two options are permanently closed when a man is joined to a woman in marriage?

   - What problems arise when these options are not closed in the mind of either the husband or the wife?

5. Why is trust an essential pillar in the foundation of a good home? What will happen without it?

6. In your opinion, which is the hardest to do, trust or be trustworthy? Why?

7. How could a lack of mutual respect between a husband and wife lead to the collapse of the home?

8. What three kinds of love are essential to a marriage?

9. Do you agree that the desires for affection, romance, and sexual fulfillment are the forces that *initiate* the building process for homes? Defend your answer from Scripture.

10. What can a husband and wife do to keep *friendship love* alive in their relationship?

11. Be ready to discuss how each of the behaviors of *agape love* listed in 1 Corinthians 13:4-8 apply to home life.

Chapter 4

Jesus in the Rooms of My Home

Bible Trivia Question: Name one home in the Bible where Jesus felt most comfortable. What comes to your mind? Did anyone say "Martha's house"? Together, Martha and her sister Mary made great use of two rooms to express their love for Jesus: the kitchen and living room (Luke 10:38-42; John 12:1-8). We feel sure He loved being in both places. The Bible simply says, *"Now Jesus loved Martha and her sister and Lazarus"* (John 11:5).

Have you ever wondered if Jesus could make Himself at home in your house? As He moves from room to room is He happy with what He sees there? Would He think of your place as a little "home away from home" for Him? Is it a small taste of heaven?

In this lesson, let's think a little more literally about what happens in the various rooms of a typical house, and the difference Jesus will make on our activities and attitudes in these rooms.

In Matthew 7:24-27, Jesus makes two things very clear:

(1) **Storms will come,** and they will beat on our homes.

(2) If our homes are to withstand the storms, they must have **Jesus and His word as the foundation**.

In the parable of the *Wise and Foolish Builders,* the two houses *may have* looked exactly the same. But they weren't the same at all. Only the wise man gave great consideration to his foundation. He *dug deep* to build on Jesus (Luke 6:48). The foolish man paid little attention to Jesus, and as the kids often sing, *"the foolish man's house went splat."*

This is not just some cute kids' song. It's serious. It's real. It happens almost every day. Someone's house goes splat! To prevent a splat, Jesus will not only have to be the foundation of our homes, He must fill every room. Pleasant riches are there (Prov. 24:3-4). Let's consider two more verses on this point.

- In John 14:23, Jesus said, *"If anyone loves Me he will keep My word; and My Father will love him, and We will come to him and make Our home with him."* Jesus wants to make Himself at home in my home and your home. For Him to do that, we must first allow Him to live in our hearts.

- In Ephesians 3:17, the apostle Paul prayed for the Ephesians that *"Christ may dwell in your hearts through faith."* The word *"dwell"* means *"to take up residence."* Jesus will live in every room of the house when He lives in the heart of each family member.

Let's now go through each of the rooms in our home and look at the impact Jesus is to have there. Our goal is to ensure that our houses stand in the day of the storm. Let's begin in a room that too often is given little thought but is essential in a God-centered home. As far as importance goes, this room is paramount.

THE LIBRARY

This is the place of our minds. So much is said in Scripture about the connection between God's word and our minds (1 Pet. 1:13-16). The one book that is central to our library is **the Bible!**

Perhaps you've heard the old joke about the problem that came up one day in a courtroom; no one could find the Bible that was used to swear in witnesses. What was the solution that was suggested? *"Get a member of the church of Christ!"* You see, people used to call members of the Lord's church *"walking Bibles."* You don't hear that much anymore. On average, Christians just do not have their faces in the book as much.

We not only need to be studying the word, we must be digging deep! It's sad, but some of us hardly know enough of God's word to fill a thimble! It is only when we have a deep and thorough knowledge of God's word, and wisdom to apply it to our lives, that we will gain the full benefit of having God's book in our homes. When the Bible is preeminent in our Library...

- **It will keep us out of trouble**. There are so many people getting into such big messes, largely because they didn't know where the dead-end roads were. The word of God gives us a jump on that (Prov. 13:13).

- **It will protect us against Satan's attacks** (Matt. 4:1-11). You cannot fight with what you don't possess. Satan loves it when he keeps us out of the word. *This book will keep you from sin, or sin will keep you from this book.*

- **It will keep us calm and steady** (Isa. 26:3). There is a lot of truth in the old saying that *"A Bible that is falling apart usually belongs to someone who isn't."* How's your Bible holding up? How are you holding up?

THE FAMILY ROOM

As we move into the family room, we should find a place where families can relax, be themselves, talk, and enjoy each other's company. Everyday problems are discussed and solved. In fact, *problems* are seen as *opportunities* to pray and discuss God's solutions. What a great place to build trust in God for guiding our lives!

It's a place where games are played together, plans are discussed, and comfort is derived just from simply being together. Family devotions and Bible discussions occur. The word of God is

35

frequently taught and discussed —sometimes more than others, but always taught (Deut. 6:6-9). God is the atmosphere of this room. Spiritual dynasties begin here—you, your son, your grandson (Deut. 6:2), and Jesus feels right at home.

Yet, this room has come under siege. A stranger has been invited into this room, corrupting our minds. His initials are T.V. **Recreation and worldly entertainment are killing spirituality!!** Kids are *zipping* through this room as they rush from one activity to the next. If they stay for any extended time, it is just to stare *zombie-like* at the television. **Computers and video games** suck time away, leaving no place in the family schedule for meaningful interaction with each other. Some of these things may not be sinful; they just choke out the word. They choke out Jesus (cf. Mt. 13:22).

Dining Room / Kitchen

One preacher told about a sad moment in his life. After his mother died, the children kept what they could from her possessions and decided to sell the rest. The one piece of furniture they reluctantly put in the yard sale was the family dinner table. Even though it was placed in the yard sale, he inwardly wished it wouldn't be bought by anyone. The table sat untouched for almost the entire day. But in the last few minutes, a man came and asked, "How much will you take for this table?" In his heart the preacher groaned but gave a price, and the table was sold. After he watched it being loaded and then carried away in the back of a truck, he went inside the house and cried. So many meals and fond memories had been made there; Sunday dinners and holiday feasts helped make a lot of those memories, but many were made during simple daily meals.

I wonder how many children today would cry if their kitchen table was taken away. How often do we even gather at our tables? Here is a great place for a little morning devotional or prayer, and for a good send-off to school. Here is a place to fill our stomachs with food and our hearts with love when we come to the end of a busy day in service to our King.

Maybe it is here that we can stop to think about the need to control our *appetites* as well. Not just our appetite for food, but our desire for prestige, success, money, material things, worldly pleasures, and lusts. These appetites can cause us to become sick with "affluenza" and addicted to work (workaholics). They create stress, cause conflicts, and lead to isolation. The wise man said, *"Better is a little with the fear of the LORD, than great treasure with trouble"* (Prov. 15:16). Just consider this. Jesus sits in the dining room of your life—the place where He sees your appetites. Is He comfortable here? Is He pleased?

THE BEDROOMS

Let's first consider the husband and wife's bedroom. This room was meant by God to be a beautiful room where a husband and wife celebrate all they share together (Heb. 13:4). What happens here is not nasty; it's holy. It's not shameful; it's lovely.

We'll discuss the physical and spiritual relationship between husband and wife in other lessons, but let's just say here that this room must not be allowed to become only a room where we collapse from fatigue and drift into sleep (1 Cor. 7:2-5).

We have a *responsibility* here, and we are asking for trouble if this room is not *nourished* and *protected*. Sweet nothings, love notes, phone calls, and compliments that occur in other rooms throughout the day keep this room vibrant and alive. Men especially need to learn this. All of these are the romantic things that create a great atmosphere for the love that is later expressed in this room.

It's also important to learn to settle any conflicts you may have as a couple before you go into this room. Pick a good time to talk, listen, make corrections, and forgive. *"Do not let the sun go down on your wrath"* (Eph. 4:26). Keep this room a room of celebration.

As we step into kids' bedrooms, we see there is much to consider here. These should be rooms of comfort and rest for children. They should be made to feel safe here. They are rooms where mom and dad are welcomed, whether it's to tuck in little children and tell a bedtime Bible story, or to sit and talk with an adolescent child about some drama unfolding among friends at school.

Here, a school-aged child might do homework, learn to play an instrument, read a book, or play with toys. And while a child should be allowed to enjoy some private time in this room, its content and activities should be monitored by parents. Is there any such thing as a parent "invading the privacy" of a child when parents are responsible for the training and well-being of their children according to both man's laws and God's law (Eph. 6:4)?

As much as we may dislike it, this room is often the room of corrective discipline. Did your parents ever say, "Go to your room"? That normally meant that some form of discipline was coming. None of us ever enjoyed the corrective discipline that happened there, but as time goes on, we are thankful. We see the peaceable fruit it brought to our lives (Heb. 12:11). Parents can rest well in later years, not worrying about where their children are and what they are doing (Prov. 29:17). As one man said after punishing his child, "Sometimes I have to break his little heart, so that when he grows up, he will not break mine." This is the admonishment of scripture: *"The rod and reproof give wisdom, but a child left to himself brings shame to his mother"* (Prov. 29:15).

THE CLOSET

Maybe here is a good place to ask, *"Is there anything in your closet?"* You can't keep it hidden. It'll torture you as long as you try to conceal it. Consider King David. While he tried to keep his sin with Bathsheba hidden, he was absolutely miserable. He knew he wasn't right with God (Psa. 32:3-5; Prov. 28:13). The only thing that brought relief was coming out of the closet, confessing his sin, and restoring his relationship with God.

Don't you think Jesus can see in your closet? He sees perfectly and even has night vision (Psa. 139:7-12). A day is coming when everything in our closet will be revealed (Eccl. 12:14).

Don't use closets to hide bad things, literally or spiritually. If you really want to hide your sin, hide it in the forgiveness of God. Let God cover it (Rom. 4:7-8). Use your closet to reveal all your weakness to God (Mt. 6:6). Pray humbly and fervently for mercy and forgiveness there.

"DOES JESUS LIVE HERE?"

For many years we've seen the following story circulated in church bulletins. Its original source and historical accuracy are unknown, but it surely makes you think!

> *The continued knock brought the mother to the door. A child stood there with a Bible in his hand. Without a word of introduction he asked, "Does Jesus live here?"*
>
> *The woman, although a member of the church, was so taken aback by the unexpected question that she did not answer. She didn't even remember what he said next, but watched him slowly walk away. All day the question kept going through her mind.*
>
> *That evening when her husband came home, she told him about it. He laughed and said, "Why didn't you show him the church directory with our name in it? You could have told him that we nearly always send our children to Bible class and go sometimes ourselves. Why didn't you remind him we give occasionally to the church, and look upon ourselves as a respected Christian family?"*
>
> *"Yes," she said, "that is all true, and I could have told him all that. But he didn't ask me the things you mentioned. He asked me if Jesus lives here, and I have been wondering all day if He does."*

The behaviors and activities that occur in the rooms of a home are the clearest indicators of whether or not Jesus dwells there. We need to let Him in. He is knocking on the door of our hearts.

In Revelation 3:20, He says, *"Behold, I stand the door and knock. If anyone hears My voice and opens the door, I will come in to him and dine with him and he with me."* That verse has been used often in extending an invitation to non-Christians to open their hearts to the Lord. You may be startled to realize that it was not written to non-Christians. It was written to Christians. How sad that we are the ones who often shut Him out of our lives. Let's decide today to open the door to Him.

> *"Let Him in, ere He is gone.*
> *Let Him in, the Holy One.*
> *Jesus Christ, the Father's Son.*
> *Let the Savior in, O let the Savior in."*
> *-- Jonathan Atchinson*

QUESTIONS

1. What is the key to building homes that will stand in the storms?

2. How can we ensure that Jesus dwells in us and in our homes (John 14:23; Eph. 3:17)?

3. What are some of the benefits of allowing the Bible to occupy the library of our minds?

4. How should we view problems that come up in the family room?

5. In what way is the family room "under siege" in modern society?

6. Is the dining room/kitchen just a place to be concerned about our appetite for food? What else can and should be going on in this room?

7. What are some things that husbands and wives can do outside of the bedroom that keep their relationship in that room alive and vibrant?

8. Should kids have *total privacy* in their bedrooms? Why or why not?

9. What will be the result of hiding things in our closets?

10. Besides storing clothes, what should we use our closets for?

Chapter 5

Constructing the Husband

———————•◉•———————

There was a man who had a little boy that he loved very much. Every day after work the man would come home and play with the little boy. He would always spend all of his extra time playing.

One night, while the man was at work, he realized that he had extra work to do for the evening and wouldn't be able to play with his son. But, he wanted to be able to give the boy something to keep him busy. So, looking around his office, he saw a magazine with a large map of the world on the cover. He got an idea. He removed the map and then patiently tore it up into small pieces. Then he put all the pieces in his coat pocket.

When he got home, the little boy came running to him and was ready to play. The man explained that he had extra work to do and couldn't play just now, but he led the little boy into the dining room, and taking out all the pieces of the map, he spread them on the table. He explained that it was a map of the world, and that by the time the boy could put it back together, his extra work would be finished, and they could both play. Surely this would keep the child busy for hours, he thought.

About half an hour later the boy came to the man and said, "Okay, it's finished. Can we play now?"

The man was surprised, saying, "That's impossible. Let's go see." And sure enough, there was the picture of the world, all put together, every piece in its place.

The man said, "That's amazing! How did you do that?" The boy said, "It was simple. On the back of the page was a picture of a man. **When I put the man together, the whole world fell into place.**"

GET YOURSELF TOGETHER!

The story above, written by an unknown author, speaks to the very point we need to make in this chapter. We are living in a day when men truly need to be "put together." The world has worked so aggressively to redefine manhood, and the result is that men are torn and confused. God has painted a picture of a true man in His word, but the world has tried to take that picture and tear it to bits. When a man tries to put himself together according to the God-given picture, the world says, "No. No. That's all wrong." Even TV sitcoms about families make the dad look goofy and incapable of leading.

This torn man has led to a torn and confused society. *How directionless we are!* We simply must get the man put together according to God's original construction. It's the only way for the world and especially our homes to "fall into place." You cannot tamper with God's design for men and women and expect the world to run fluidly.

Our current situation is much like the shambled society to which Ezekiel preached. He said, *"So, I sought for man...but I found no one"* (Ezek. 22:30). How sad! A man was needed, but one could not be found.

We love the words of Gianna Jessen, a late-term abortion survivor, who in a speech to the Australian Parliament said...

"For just a brief moment,
I would like to speak directly to the men
in this room and do something that is never done.
Men, you are made for greatness.
You are made to stand up and be men.
You are made to defend women and children.
Not stand by and turn your head when you
know murder is occurring and do nothing about it.
You are not made to use women and leave us alone.
You are made to be **kind and great and gracious and strong**
and stand for something *because men, listen to me,*
I am too tired to do your job...
You are made to defend what is right and good.
This fiery young girl will stand here and say,
'Now is your moment.'
What sort of man do you want to be;
a man obsessed with your own glory,
or a man obsessed with the glory of God?"

So, let's pick up the pieces and begin to put them in place so that we might have the man, and more specifically, the husband and father God wanted us to have.

THE PIECES THAT MAKE A GODLY HUSBAND

The Bible word that best speaks to the leadership of the husband and father is "head." Christ is the *pattern* of headship for the husband. As head of the church, Christ has *"preeminence"* in *all things* (Col. 1:18). Preeminence means to be "first in rank and influence" *(Strong's Hebrew/Greek Dictionary)*. The husband should also have the place of preeminence in the home. He has first sought to put himself together in such a way as to be a little replica of Christ in the home. He wants to do things "just as" Christ would do it. Notice how often the words "just as" and "as" are used in Ephesians 5:22-33 to emphasize this truth.

So, in general, man is the head of woman (1 Cor. 11:3). As it relates to the home, God has said, *"The husband is head of the wife, as also Christ is head of the church; and He is the Savior of the body"* (Eph. 5:23). It seems that some people think that this idea of the man being the head of the home went out in the 1950's with hula hoops. But it's as old as the creation of the world, and was determined by God Himself (Gen. 3:16). How did God come to make that decision? Scripture says it was based on the order of their creation and Eve's transgression in the garden (1 Tim. 2:11-15).

Regrettably, too many men are eager to seize upon this concept as God-given authority for them to assume the position of power in the home—often for their own selfish ends—to get their way, to fulfill their desire for pleasure, and to silence the sincere concerns and criticisms expressed by their wives.

Many times the *so-called head* of a family is little more than a *selfish tyrant* full of wants, demands, and wishes, with little self-control or concern for the needs of others. Perhaps this all-too-common spirit of selfish dominance explains some of the backlash from society against male leadership. But the existence of husbands and fathers who do things wrong doesn't prove that God's plan is wrong. It just proves that men sin! Don't throw the baby out with the bathwater. Just get it right. No self-absorbed, self-serving man can ever be the husband God designed. He must alter his concept of headship to coincide with what is revealed in Scripture.

Christ *never* used His preeminence as justification for being self-serving. Rather, He sacrificed Himself so that the church might have every need supplied and *"grow up in all things into Him who is the head; Christ"* (Eph. 4:7-15). Self-sacrificial love is the first obligation of a husband's headship. Husbands are to *"love your wives, even as Christ also loved the church, and gave himself for it"* (Eph. 5:25). And a wife and children who have had such a husband and father will tell you they are blessed indeed.

Like the *"point man"* leading his troop in war, the husband is to be trained in the boot camp of God's word to lead his family in the battle for eternity (cf. Eph. 6:12). Any mistake he makes could cost them their lives. Now, that's weighty!! It is not a position to gloat in, it's a call to duty! Souls are at stake! It requires having a vision of where you want this family to go. The head is where the eyes (vision) are. It's a vision cast by God. The husband is the head of the wife, but he also has one who is Head over him – Jesus Christ! This means that final decisions in regard to the family are ultimately His to make.

Leadership

As the leader in his family, Joshua declared, *"As for me and my house, we will serve the Lord"* (Josh. 24:15). This declaration, along with Joshua's exemplary life, well illustrates the role of husband as the leader.

First, the husband is responsible to *set family goals*. The most important of these are spiritual goals, although goals relating to other matters such as the education of children and financial security also have their place. Joshua set the goal for his family– *"We will serve the Lord!"*

Second, the husband will *see to it that the activity and climate within the family correspond to the goal(s)* that have been set. If the goal is *"we will serve the Lord,"* then activities like church attendance, Bible study, prayer, and helping others will be a consistent part of daily family life. The climate or atmosphere within the family will be conducive to serving the Lord.

Third, the *example* set by the husband will serve to reinforce the goal(s). Christ served as the perfect example for the body of which He is the head (cf. 1 Pet. 2:21-22). Everyone under the headship of Christ can look to Him as an example of how to achieve the goals He has set for us. He is a true *Captain* or leader of our salvation (Heb. 2:10). Likewise, the husband who has declared *serving the Lord* to be a family goal must also lead by example. If he fails to attend worship services or pray, cusses at his wife, has beer in the refrigerator, etc., he is NOT behaving as a leader. Similarly, the husband who has set certain financial goals for the family, yet squanders a large portion of his paycheck on frivolous items, is NOT behaving as a leader.

Direction

Headship also involves direction. The head of a body directs the movement of the body; it tells the body what to do! The fact that wives are commanded to be subject to and obedient to their husbands necessarily implies that their husbands are to give directions or commands (Eph. 5:24; Titus 2:5).

Direction involves two things: determining what needs to be done and communicating it to the one who needs to do it. Many men have problems with one or both of these. Determining what needs to be done is a decision-making process. If a man considers only his own needs and wants, poor decisions will be made. Since good decisions require consideration of the needs of others (discussed below) and correspondence to the goals of the family (discussed above), many men are not good decision-makers. Some avoid it altogether. In so doing they abdicate their headship.

Even if the husband makes a good decision, he may not communicate it well. Such a husband is like the head of a paraplegic who has had the nerve connections between his legs and head damaged or destroyed. It makes no difference what the head determines the legs should do; the legs will not comply because the message is never communicated. Many wives suffer from constantly having to guess as to the will of their husbands. If they guess wrong, they are blamed. But the real blame belongs to the husband who has failed to be the head by giving inadequate direction.

Elders who rule in the churches are held out to us in Scripture as being ideal Christian men whose faith is worthy of imitation (cf. Heb. 13:7). 1 Timothy 3:4 teaches that one qualification to be an elder in the church is that a man *"rules his own house well."* The word translated "rule" in this passage (Gr. *proistemi*) means "to be at the head, rule, direct" (Bauer, *A Greek-English Lexicon*, p. 707). Every Christian man should determine to rule his house well by clearly communicating well-thought-out directions to each member of his household.

Consideration

One of the most challenging tasks faced by the head of the family is the responsibility to give due consideration to the needs of those who are under him. A husband who is truly functioning as the head of his wife *"nourishes and cherishes"* her as his *"own"* body (Eph. 5:28-29).

This demands that the husband be as much aware of his wife's needs as he is his own. He must dwell with his wife *"with understanding, giving honor to the wife as to the weaker vessel"* (1 Peter 3:7). The phrase *"with understanding"* (from the Greek word *gnosis*—*"to know"*) suggests that the husband thoroughly *knows* his wife. When the Bible says to treat her as the weaker vessel, it is not demeaning her strength. The husband knows the special physical and emotional constitution of his wife, which is at once more beautiful and more delicate than his own. Just like a piece of fine china is wrapped in bubble wrap because of its great value, so the wife is wrapped in the considerate love of her husband because she is valuable to him and the family. He comprehends the unique needs of a *vessel* which is weaker.

This understanding that a husband has of his wife will have many applications. In practical terms, it will mean that he considers her need for affectionate reassurance as he interacts with her throughout the day. It will mean that he considers the monthly cycle of his wife before approaching her for sex. And it will mean that he considers her need for adult conversation before he tunes her out and tunes in the TV. Most importantly, it will mean listening to her and really considering what she has to say.

There is wisdom in the latter. A wife has eyes that can see what the husband doesn't, a mind that assimilates information in a different way, a heart with sensitivities that the man may not possess, and strengths that offset his weaknesses. Like pilot and copilot, the plane ride will be much smoother if they communicate effectively, accurately and respectfully. In the cockpit of home and family, husbands and wives must remember they are working together in the most crucial flight of all—they are trying to navigate a marriage and a family in the direction of heaven. This is not a job for kids. It's a job for mature adults.

One great Bible example of a time when a man did well to listen is when David was about to kill the husband of Abigail—a decision he was sure to regret. Abigail, as a wise woman, helped David to think long-term and make a better decision. He saw in her these great traits of wisdom and later married her (1 Sam. 25:32-35).

In the relationship of the church to Christ, does the Lord allow us to express our wishes? Of course He does! It sometimes changes His mind (James 5:16-18). Sometimes it doesn't (2 Cor. 12:7-10). But always, He considers us and does what is best for us.

Failing to understand the needs and appreciate the contributions of a wife may result in a husband becoming bitter toward his wife. He may regard her as a source of irritation rather than a treasure to be carefully nourished and maintained. This attitude is in *direct disobedience* to God's command to husbands to *be not bitter toward* their wives (Col. 3:19). Such bitterness is SINFUL!!

The root of the problem is in the failure to "love" and "honor" the wife. Honor means to value or esteem highly. When a husband ignores his wife's words, feelings, thoughts, and opinions, he is not valuing his wife. He is effectively dishonoring her. He is sinning and needs to repent.

Provision

God's word teaches that one who does not *"provide for his own ...household"* has *"denied the faith and is worse than an unbeliever"* (1 Tim. 5:8). One definition of the word "provide" is to "supply what is needed"*(Webster's 7th Collegiate Dictionary)*. As the head of the wife, it is the husband's duty and privilege to *provide* for the wife's needs. What are these needs?

Physical needs are the most obvious ones. God's curse upon man that he would eat *"in toil"* and in *"the sweat of your face"* suggests that it is man's responsibility to work to provide for physical necessities (Gen. 3:17-19). The duty of working to provide for his family's food, shelter, and clothing is placed primarily upon the husband in Scripture. The modern trend of women having careers outside the home not only hinders wives from fulfilling their duties in the home, it may also undercut one of the primary headship functions of the husband.

Another physical need of the wife is the sexual need. As has been mentioned, husbands have an obligation to fulfill this need. 1 Corinthians 7:1-5 has as much to say about the husband rendering *"affection"* and giving up *"authority over his own body"* as it does about the wife doing so. The sexual experience enjoyed by the bride in the Song of Solomon should be the experience of every woman whose husband is fulfilling his role as head (Song 2:3-6).

The spiritual needs of the wife must also be provided for by the husband. Godly wives have a keen interest in spiritual things. They want and need someone who is an *"heir together of the grace of life"*: Someone who will pray with them and for them (1 Peter 3:7); someone who will go with them to church, and who will be concerned with their salvation (Acts 10:24); and someone who is capable of answering their questions about spiritual matters (1 Cor. 14:35).

The emotional needs of a wife are typically more unlike those of the husband than any others. Husbands must work to understand and fulfill these needs. Many of these needs can be fulfilled if the husband will but heed the command to *honor* his wife (1 Peter 3:7).

The husband of a worthy woman honors her by praising her (Prov. 31:28-29). He displays his affection for her as Isaac showed *"endearment to Rebekah his wife"* (Gen. 26:8). He *cherishes* his wife (Eph. 5:29). The Greek word translated "cherishes" *(Gr. thalpo)* in this text originally meant "to keep warm, as of birds covering their young with feathers." It is being used figuratively in

Ephesians 5:29, signifying "to cherish with tender love, to foster with tender care." *(W.E. Vine's Expository Dictionary, p. 186).*

Here then are the pieces lying on the table. Every piece is needed to put the husband and father together. Envision a puzzle box in front of you as a guide. The box is God's word. It shows a grand picture of how this godly man in the home will look when you are done. Put him together, and rest assured that when you do, your home will fall right into place.

In future lessons, we'll discuss more fully the needs of both husbands and wives. The critical point to remember at this juncture is that, just as Christ gave Himself completely to supply every need of the church, even so, the husband must make supplying the needs of his wife his utmost concern.

QUESTIONS

1. How should the headship of the husband be like the headship of Christ over the church?

2. How are the duties and privileges of the husband summed up in the word "head"?

3. What three things does leadership demand of the husband?

4. What can husbands learn from Christ about leading by example?

5. What two things does *giving direction* involve?

6. Why is it difficult for many husbands to do a good job as the decision-making head?

7. Describe the process a husband should go through in making decisions.

8. An elder must be a man *who "rules his own house well"* (1 Tim. 3:7). Is it right to hold other Christian husbands to this same standard? Why or why not?

9. Does God demand that the husband be as much aware of his wife's needs as he is of his own? Defend your answer from Scripture.

10. What specific, practical things can a husband do to gain an *understanding* of his wife and her needs?

11. What spiritual needs do wives have which husbands can help fulfill?

12. List at least five specific things a husband can do to *give honor* to his wife.

Chapter 6

Constructing the Wife

Many women may *groan in their spirits* as they read what we assert in the following sentence:

> **The key** *to building a wife*
> *who meets with God's design specifications*
> *may be found in an understanding of the word* **subjection.**

Some women may feel that they have already been beaten over the head by husbands and preachers with the concept of subjection. Others in our feminist culture may resent the very idea of subjection.

One example of our society's distaste for the Bible's teaching on the subject was seen in the criticism the Southern Baptist Convention received in 1998 when it voted overwhelmingly to add four paragraphs about the nature of the family to the "Baptist Faith and Message," the central statement of the denomination's beliefs, which had not been amended for 35 years. What statement caused such a stir? It was this:

> *"A wife is to submit herself graciously*
> *to the servant leadership of her husband*
> *even as the church willingly submits*
> *to the headship of Christ."*

While we do not endorse man-made conventions, synods, or councils, we do believe the reactions of people are noteworthy. Some years later, former president Jimmy Carter, a Baptist himself, spoke out on the statement and withdrew himself from the Convention. We have highlighted in bold print something we wish to emphasize. In an interview with *TIME Magazine* Carter said...

> *"As you may or may not know,*
> *the Southern Baptist Convention*
> *back now about 13 years ago in Orlando,*
> ***voted that women were inferior***
> *and had to be subservient to their husbands,*
> *and ordained that a woman could not be a deacon or a pastor*
> *or a chaplain or even a teacher in a classroom in some seminaries*
> *where men are in the classroom, boys are in the classroom."*[6]

Women are inferior? From where did the President get that? That was **never said** in the statement. And neither is it ever said in the Bible, our only God-given guide in matters regarding the family. But that's what people think is being said, and that's what gets some people "all bristled up."

ARE WE UNDERSTANDING SUBMISSION?

It is also doubtful that very many Christians (men or women) have a good working idea of what subjection involves or why it is so vital in building good homes. In practice, there is probably *almost as much* lack of subjection on the part of wives as there is failure in headship on the part of husbands. Nonetheless, *subjection* or *submission* is the key to constructing a good wife.

The subjection of wives to husbands is *repeatedly* emphasized in scripture. In Ephesians 5:22-24 wives are told to *"submit to your own husbands as to the Lord"* and that *"just as the church is subject to Christ, so let the wives be to their own husbands in everything"* (Col. 3:18). Younger wives are to be instructed to be

---

[6] Quoted by Eric Stirgus, www.politifact.com, Friday, June 28, 2013.

"obedient to their own husbands" (Titus 2:5). Peter instructs wives to *"be in subjection to your own husbands"* (1 Peter 3:1, KJV).

Obviously, if the Lord thought it was important to repeatedly emphasize His desire that wives be in subjection to their husbands, it would be very unwise for any wife who is trying to be what God designed her to be in the home to refuse to embrace this concept.

Submission recognizes God's chain of command. The words *"subjection," "obedient," "submit,"* and *"subject"* in the verses cited above are all translations of a single Greek word *(hupotasso)*. This word was "primarily a military term" meaning "to rank under" *(Vine's Expository Dictionary)*. "Originally it is a hierarchical term which stresses the relation to superiors" or what we might call a chain of command. In these passages, "the issue is keeping a divinely-willed order" *(Theological Dictionary of the New Testament, vol. 8, pp. 41 & 43)*.

Human relationships have been designed by God to work best when His order is respected and maintained. It is important to realize that one's place in God's chain of command is not necessarily determined by ability, intelligence, or worth.

Even Jesus Christ, the Lord of glory, was "subject" to His earthly parents, not because He was an inferior being, but because that was the way God ordered the home (Luke 2:51). For that matter, Jesus was subject to His heavenly Father, but He was never inferior (John 5:30). In fact, He was equal with the Father (John 5:18ff). It is when you have equals that submission becomes truly necessary. Furthermore, it is for the purpose of maintaining God's order that citizens are to be subject to government, slaves to masters, and the church to Christ (1 Peter 2:13; 3:18-20; Eph. 5:22-24). Wives must see subjection as compliance to God's orderly design. God's book promotes this viewpoint by pointing out that a wife's subjection to her husband is *parallel* to the subjection of the church to Christ (Eph. 5:22-24).

Notice also that, as the church submits to Christ, wives are to submit to their husbands *"in everything"* (Eph. 5:24). No part of the husband's expressed will is to be rejected by the wife **unless** it would involve her in disobedience to Christ (Acts 5:29). Just as we in the church must do what Christ wants done and not what we might personally prefer to do, the wife must also do as her husband directs.

Simply put, subjection shouldn't be so hard to understand. We do it every day at our jobs, in schools, within the military, etc. Two people also do it when they ride the same horse. If two people ride the same horse, somebody has to sit up front!! This is not rocket science. It's fundamental and understandable.

ATTITUDES PROMOTING SUBMISSION

Some wives find subjection to be very difficult. It is not easy to place oneself totally under the authority of another. But God has given wives several good reasons to do so. Wives would do well to study and meditate on these God-given reasons to submit to their husbands (cf. Psa. 119:15, 48).

(1) **A desire to obey Christ.** Wives are to submit to their husbands *"as to the Lord"* (Eph. 5:22). Obedience or disobedience to a husband is obedience or disobedience to Christ.

(2) **A concern for what is appropriate behavior before the world.** It is *"fitting in the Lord"* for a wife to submit to her husband (Col. 3:18). "Fitting" refers to what is proper. Even people of the world do not view a self-willed, over-bearing wife as truly representing Christianity. The title character on the old sitcom *Roseanne* was just such a character; a lot of people thought she was funny, but nobody thought she was a Christian. Men who are not Christians may get negative impressions of Christianity when they see believing wives who will not submit. For this reason, the Bible says that wives are to be *"obedient to their own husbands, that the word of God may not be blasphemed"* (Titus 2:5).

(3) Love. Women who love their husbands and love their children (Titus 2:4) will want the best for them. The believing wife knows that God's way is best.

(4) Respect. In Ephesians 5:33, the wife is told to *"see that she respects her husband."* Holy women of old who were in subjection to their husbands maintained this attitude and expressed it. Abraham's wife Sarah expressed her respect for him by calling him "lord" (1 Peter 3:5-6). Even if a husband is not a man of faith like Abraham, he should still be able to observe an attitude of respect *("fear")* in his wife (1 Peter 3:2). A wife who does not respect her husband in mind and word will simply find it impossible to submit herself to him as she should.

(5) A desire to make home life better. Women typically express more concern than men for making their home life better. When this desire is coupled with the realization that improvement *must begin* with oneself, a woman has a strong motivation to submit to her husband. The result is so powerful that it *can even* win an unbelieving husband to Christ (1 Peter 3:1).

(6) Meekness. The *"meek and quiet spirit"* with which women are to adorn themselves also promotes subjection (1 Peter 3:4). R.C. Trench has said that meekness "is that temper of spirit in which we accept His [God's] dealings with us as good, and therefore without disputing or resisting." A meek person *could* resist or dispute, but when confronted with God's will, he or she chooses not to. Aristotle used the term to describe a horse which had been broken and willingly submitted to reins in its master's hand. Wives who have adorned themselves with meekness will be able to submit to good husbands and bad ones, just as servants with the same attitude are to submit not only to *"good and gentle"* masters *"but also to the harsh"* (1 Peter 2:18).

(7) An understanding of the purpose of subjection—to be a helper. Subjection is not an end in itself. God has placed

woman under man for a reason. She was created to occupy
this position, and in it she can best fulfill her role as a
"helper" (1 Cor. 11:9-10; Gen. 2:18; 1 Tim. 2:12-13). The
wife should want to accept her rank under her husband
because only there can she fulfill God's purpose for her.

BECOMING A HELPER

If *head* is the one word which best describes the place of the
husband in the home, then perhaps the one word which best
describes the wife's place in the home is *help.* It was God's
intention in creating woman to create *"a helper suitable"* for man
(Gen. 2:18, NIV). God has revealed specifically how she is to
assist. The wife is to *help* by...

(1) Bearing children. From the beginning, God's desire for
humans was that they be "fruitful and multiply" (Gen.
1:28). Obviously, men cannot accomplish this alone. God
designed women with the physical and mental tools to bear
and nurture children. This is such a vital part of God's
intention for women that in 1 Timothy 5:14 God's word
actually *instructs* younger widows to marry and *"bear
children."*

(2) Providing companionship and affection. Men, despite
their gruff exteriors, need and crave companionship and
affection. It is not good for a man to be alone, and a wife
was created to be that needed companion (Gen. 2:18; Mal.
2:14). A wife is not just to be someone who is *there with*
her husband, but someone who provides him with needed
love and affection (Titus 2:4). She offers her husband
praise, encouragement, and emotional support.

(3) Fulfilling sexual needs. As was mentioned in a previous
lesson, the husband is to look to his wife for fulfillment of
his sexual needs (Prov. 5:15-20; Song of Sol. 5:10-16).
Since the wife alone can lawfully fulfill these needs, the
woman who truly loves her husband will make every effort

to keep him satisfied. From a Biblical standpoint, by doing this she *helps* him avoid the temptation of fornication (1 Cor. 7:1-5).

(4) Maintaining chastity and purity. Wives are commanded to be *"chaste"* (Titus 2:5; 1 Peter 3:2). This word refers to being modest or pure from carnality. Husbands need wives as sexual partners whose conduct out of the bedroom reinforces the undefiled nature of their physical relationship (cf. Heb. 13:4). Such a wife not only helps her husband maintain a wholesome view of sex, but by her example she also helps him to strive to maintain a high standard of personal morality—he is less likely to sully himself with worldliness because he wants to stay pure for her.

(5) Being spiritually-minded. The spiritual attitude and behavior of the wife has an impact on her husband. Women from Eve to Jezebel and on down to the present have influenced their husbands to commit evil. But a woman who adorns herself with a meek and quiet spirit and behaves as a Christian should can influence even the worst men for good (1 Peter 3:1-2). Husbands need such an influence. Many will not get to heaven without it.

(6) Keeping the home. Wives are to be *homemakers*— literally "workers at home" (Titus 2:5). But that is not to say that the wife is simply to be a maid, nor should she be viewed as such by her husband. God's will is also that wives *"guide"* or *"manage the house"* (1 Timothy 5:14, KJV & NKJV). The wife helps the husband by being the working manager of household affairs. Proverbs 31:10-31 gives a detailed description of what such a wife did in Biblical times. Thus, wives' duties in the home are not merely menial, but require management skills such as planning and decision-making. Any husband blessed with a wife who so runs the household knows what a help it is to him.

The goal of a wife is to bring honor to her husband, just as the goal of the church is to bring glory to Christ. This is not really a specific activity that a wife engages in, but the result of all her other efforts to help her husband. Because she is such a help, *"her husband is known in the gates when he sits among the elders of the land"* (Prov. 31:23). When a wife lives for the glory of her husband, her own value becomes incalculable, her beauty unfading, and her praise heartfelt and lavish (Prov. 31:10, 28-31; 1 Peter 3:4-6).

Proverbs 12:4 states that *"An excellent wife is the crown of her husband...."* The crown is obviously a symbol of glory and honor. The man who finds such a wife *"finds a good thing, and obtains favor from the LORD"* (Prov. 18:22).

QUESTIONS

1. List all of the scriptures you can find in the New Testament which address the subject of a wife's responsibility to her husband but fail to mention subjection, submission, or obedience.

2. Define *subjection*.

3. In what way or ways is the wife's subjection to her husband to be like the subjection of the church to Christ?

4. What impressions might an unsubmissive wife leave on non-Christians?

5. What should a wife do if she is having trouble respecting her husband?

6. How will a meek spirit help a woman be in subjection to her husband, even if he is not a particularly good husband?

7. For what purpose have wives been placed in subjection to their husbands?

8. Do you agree that one way wives help their husbands is by offering them praise and emotional support?

   • What are some things for which wives can praise their husbands?

   • How would this help the husband?

9. Is there ever a circumstance in which it would be appropriate for a wife to feel that she is partially to blame for her husband committing fornication? (Defend your answer from Scripture.)

10. How is lewd public behavior or immodest dress on the part of a wife harmful to a husband?

11. RESEARCH: List at least two Bible examples of wives who were a good influence on their husbands and two that were an evil influence.

12. Be prepared to discuss Proverbs 31:10-31. Specifically, how was this *worthy woman* a help to her husband?

Chapter 7

Husbands and Wives
Understanding Each Other's Needs

Like so many couples, when Easton and Reagan married, they felt as if they were enjoying life on the grand level of most fairy tales...like Cinderella or something. But after the bells stopped ringing, the bills started calling. They had lots of those. They maxed credit cards, got a bank loan, and secured a hefty mortgage in order to have right away what mom and dad had achieved after many years.

They both took to their jobs, and soon tensions began to build like they do in a lot of homes. Easton became a workaholic, gradually finding his identity in his work. Reagan worked but not so enjoyably because her feminine wiring didn't quit firing when she got home. She still had meals to cook, laundry to wash, a house to clean, etc., etc., etc. It became even more hectic after their first child was born.

All the while, Easton and Reagan were losing touch with each other. They seldom had meaningful conversation; they fought often, and on weekends spent time with their friends but seldom one-to-one with each other. But still Easton thought, "Isn't this the way most marriages are?" He intended to do better and had plans to do just that, but it seemed to him he was stuck on an uphill escalator from which he couldn't step off. What he didn't realize was that he was really on an escalator of a marriage headed down.

It hit the bottom floor the day Reagan walked in and said, "I'm not happy. I want a divorce." Easton was shocked beyond imagination. What he didn't know was that in the last few months while he was not meeting Reagan's needs, there was someone at work who was more than happy to put a smile on her face.

Another dispute in court was coming, all because of unmet needs.

Get this lesson. Download it. Hardwire it. Burn it on the brain. Husbands and wives each have unique needs; if those needs are unmet, it usually spells D-I-V-O-R-C-E. Unmet needs do not justify divorce, but they often produce it.

To us, the diamond of all marriage scriptures is 1 Peter 3:7. We have **printed in bold text** some of the words for our focus.

> *Husbands, likewise, **dwell with them with understanding**,*
> *giving honor to the wife, as to the weaker vessel,*
> *and as being heirs together of the grace of life,*
> *that your prayers may not be hindered.*

This verse is instructing husbands to dwell with their wives with *"understanding"* or *"according to knowledge."* While this verse is speaking to husbands, it has application to wives as well. The verse teaches that husbands are to know or understand their wives. Be each other's study project. Learn the needs of the one you married, see how God uniquely wired him or her, and determine to meet those needs. Bluntly stated, "It's not about you!" Both the man and woman are unique because of God's design. It takes much effort to understand one another, but this you must do!! Fail to do it, and you might buy yourself Easton and Reagan's problems.

When God said He made us male and female, He was saying volumes. A best-selling book title a few years ago declared that, *"Men are from Mars, Women are from Venus."* In Genesis 2:18, when God said that He intended to make a *"helper comparable"* to man, He was indicating that man and woman are vastly different, but they were meant to complete one another. The word translated *comparable* in that text could literally be rendered *"the opposite part."* God created man and woman to be dissimilar in many respects, precisely so the two could become one. He made them to fit one another like puzzle pieces in a beautiful portrait.

Let's now stroll down the road that reveals some of the commonly found needs of husbands and wives.

WHAT HUSBANDS NEED

Some time ago, Willard Harley wrote a very popular book called *His Needs, Her Needs.* In his survey of men, he found 5 common things that men listed as their needs. Here are his findings.[7]

(1) **Sexual Fulfillment**
(2) **Recreational Companionship**
(3) **An attractive spouse**
(4) **Domestic Support**
(5) **Admiration**

As we have stated in previous lessons, God knows us better than we know ourselves, and he knows what our true needs are. Now, these findings may not match you or your mate perfectly. The point—find out what *your* mate's needs are and meet them.

Sexual Fulfillment. In simple and straightforward words, a typical man feels a deep need to make love to his wife. If he senses no passion in her for him sexually, he ends up very, very tense and frustrated. One man writes through his depression and says, "A marriage without sex makes me feel unappreciated. I'm a plumber, electrician, handyman, groundskeeper, taxi driver, moneybag, childcare giver, and roommate. But I no longer feel like a husband. I tried flowers, notes, and romantic candlelit

---

[7] Willard F. Harley, Jr., *His Needs, Her Needs*, (Grand Rapids, MI: Fleming H. Revell, 2001).

dinners. I couldn't sleep, and most important, I couldn't sleep with my wife."

We are shocked and disturbed greatly and a bit surprised when young couples are having issues in the bedroom. This we know for certain: God's will is for the marital bedroom to be a celebration of all a spiritual husband and wife are (Prov. 5:18-20; Heb. 13:4), and unmet sexual needs are a recipe for disaster (1 Cor. 7:3-5). In the Corinthians passage just cited, God basically says of making love, "Do this. Don't stop. Except for a little time. And then get back to it." If you are failing here, Satan is sitting in the stands eager with bated breath to enter the game and bring a special mistress with him to be a spoiler to your marriage. Beware!!

Recreational Companionship. This is the idea of a wife supporting, encouraging, and even sharing in her husband's recreational enjoyments. Men tend to like things like sports, cars, and outdoor activities. Each man and woman is different, but it is rare that their natural interests coincide. Should a wife try to show interest in the recreational things her husband enjoys? Is there a Biblical basis for answering that question? I believe there is.

The wife is to love and respect her husband (Eph. 5:33; Titus 2:4). It is her interest in him – her respect for who he is and what he loves – that creates in her an interest in his interests. Now maybe she isn't suited to going hunting or golfing with him, and maybe it is just not in her to enjoy watching a sporting event like he does. But she can try to understand the things he enjoys, and she can adore him while he enjoys them!

We know of a man who enjoys flying. For the longest, he begged his wife to go. She was afraid and never would. Such is understandable. But one day she saw a plane that actually had a parachute...for the plane itself! She said, "Get one like that, and I'll go with you." The next thing she knew, he had one, and she found herself buckled in the passenger seat. How does he describe that moment? Listen... *"One of my biggest aspirations has been to be able to have Jeanie travel with me in our plane. When she decided to go with me, it was the most exhilarating trip ever. To know that she had the confidence in me as a pilot reiterated the trust she has had from the beginning of our relationship. I will provide and protect her at all costs. Her trust and confidence in me has built my esteem more than she will ever know. I am confident that our bond has solidified even stronger by the trust we have in each other* Eye opening isn't it? Somehow he connected that flying trip with respect for him and trust in him.

To put the shoe on the other foot, we recall the story Harry Pickup, Jr. told many years ago about going to the opera with his wife Joella. He knew little about the opera and would probably have had no inclination to go on his own, but his wife was a music teacher who loved such things. His love for her caused him to truly enjoy seeing her enjoy the experience.

An Attractive Spouse. Husbands say that they want their wives to be attractive. In bygone years, a common piece of advice for a young wife was that she should try to be especially attractive and vibrant when her husband returned home from work. Do you think that was good advice? Again, what Biblical basis could there possibly be for such counsel?

Consider this. From a Biblical viewpoint, a woman should want to please her husband. If she knows that, as a man, he is pleased with her when she looks her best, would it be considerate of her to make an effort to do so? Could she just simply strive to always be *his* beauty queen? Someone has said, *"Attractiveness is what you do with what you have."* And ask yourself this: *At every stage, as they go through life together, is there any point at which a man would not like his wife to be attractive to him?* Sarah and Rebekah must have known something about the importance of this even as they aged. They remained beautiful to their husbands (Gen.12:11-12; 26:7-8).

On a practical, albeit superficial level, we might ask if a wife should let a hairdresser talk her into a hairstyle she knows her husband will not like. Is constantly wearing old and bedraggled night clothes, curlers, and "goop" on your face at bedtime a good idea? Obviously, no person is always going to look her best, especially after a long day of seeing to the needs of children, or cleaning house, or working a secular job. But wives need to *understand* that their husbands feel that they need a wife who is attractive. And again, usually there is a woman somewhere, who during the day, looks her very best and is there for your husband to see.

Now, we think it is important for both husbands and wives to recognize that the most important kind of beauty isn't physical. A spiritual man will be very happy with a woman whose most attractive features are inward; this is the true beauty that both God and a godly man appreciate (1 Peter 3:3-4; Prov. 31:28b-30).

Domestic Support. In years gone by, it was often stressed in ladies' classes that a wife needed to have the home well-prepared and in order when her husband arrived home from work. It was emphasized that he needed a place of peace and quiet, a nest to come home to, and a place to unwind and "get away from life's stresses." A generation or two ago, even people in the world would have said that this was great advice. TV shows like *Leave it to Beaver* and *Father Knows Best* depicted just such idyllic homes.

Do you think most men today feel a need for this? You might be interested to know that research suggests that they do. Do you think this is being fulfilled in most homes today? Observation suggests that it isn't. But what does the Bible say? Does the Bible spend a lot of time stressing the need for women to be "career driven," or does it indicate that a wife's attentions should be focused on a well-run home? Where does the Bible put its emphasis for the wife and mother (Titus 2:4-5; 1 Tim. 5:14; Prov. 31)?

This is not to say that it is necessarily wrong for a wife and mother to work outside the home. There appear to be Bible examples where godly women did so, at least on a limited basis (Proverbs 31; Acts 16:14-15; 18:3). In an instance where a husband and wife are both working, there needs to be some give and take, helping to meet each other's need in the area of domestic support. If the wife is willing to work a secular job to help support the family, then it is only right that the husband make some additional sacrifices to help his wife keep the home.

Admiration. In Ephesians 5:33, the wife is told to *"respect her husband."* Good men do a lot to provide for their families, and they feel good when they are able to do it (1 Tim. 5:8). This desire can sometime lead to them becoming "workaholics." Other reasons they become workaholics are...

- *Addiction*—They find it intoxicating.
- *Identity*—That's where their self-worth is tied up.
- *Survival*—They meet with pressure from the employer.
- *Lifestyle*—It's the only way to keep up a standard of living.

Working long hours from time to time is normal, necessary, and even a healthy part of life. There are times a man just has to do it. The point here is that men value being appreciated for what they do, and it helps them keep everything in proper balance when the love and appreciation they get at home is what it ought to be.

A most touching story from years ago has been told of a man who came home to a candlelit dinner. The reason? He made so little, the wife was unable to pay the light bill. In tears she said, "You work so hard, and we're trying, but it's pretty rough. I didn't have enough money to pay the light bill. I didn't want you to know about it, so I thought we would just eat by candlelight." He told this story when the day came he preached her funeral and gave honor to her. With intense emotion, he said, "She could have broken my spirit; she could have ruined me; she could have demoralized me. But instead she said, 'Somehow or another we'll get these lights back on. But tonight let's eat by candlelight.'" [8]

---

[8] Emerson Eggerichs, *Love & Respect* (Nashville, TN: Thomas Nelson, 2004).

On the flipside of unavoidable tight budgets, some men feel unappreciated and disrespected when their efforts to provide are undermined by thoughtless and careless spending by the wife. Wives need to be careful not to let the purchase of unnecessary things be their pursuit of happiness. If we are not happy, the root is probably somewhere else, not in some new "bling, bling."

We are about to move on in this study to consider the needs of wives. One important thing to be noticed is that the needs of husbands and wives are complementary—when a husband fulfills the needs of the wife, she can better fulfill his needs, and vice versa. One of the needs of the wife is CONVERSATION. Should a husband tell his wife when she has said or done something that made him feel disrespected? Yes! Should he mention when he feels other needs are not being met? Yes! If a husband never says much about his unmet needs or her disrespectful comments and actions, should she assure herself that all is well? She can't! But she also can't be expected to *know* what those needs are until he communicates!

WHAT WIVES NEED

Harley listed the five needs of wives as follows:

(1) Affection
(2) Conversation
(3) Honesty and Openness
(4) Financial Support
(5) Family Commitment

Would most wives who are Christians agree with these five? Would they list them in the same order? Perhaps not. And perhaps they would want to add items to the list, such as *spiritual leadership*, which we will include later as part of our discussion of *family commitment*.

Do husbands *understand* that these are the needs of their wives? Often not. Men typically can perceive that their wives have needs that are not being met, but they are often baffled when it comes to identifying those needs. At this juncture, husbands need to get it settled in their minds that they *must* understand their wives (1 Peter 3:7), and determine that they *will* do what is necessary to please them! *"But he who is married cares about the things of the world—how he may please his wife"*(1 Cor. 7:33).

Affection. Remember what most men gave as their #1 need? It was sexual fulfillment. Just as this is very hard for a woman to understand about her man, it may be hard for the man to understand her need for affection. You don't have to understand *why* she has this need, but you do need to understand *that she has it*. And, you do have to know how to provide it.

For a woman, affection is the atmosphere she needs to be able to respond to the physical needs of her man. This is why a book is titled *"Sex Begins in the Kitchen."* That means sex begins for her in the warm way you greet her in the morning and the attention and affection you show her through the day. Often, what the husband thinks of as "preliminaries" are the wife's "main event" (Harley). You cannot treat her negatively during the day and expect her to have a warm desire to please you in the evening. She needs atmosphere.

Guys, affection and sex are not the same thing! A while back a woman said, *"Say romance to a man and he thinks S-E-X."* Men must learn sexless affection. Don't let this point escape you. **Many women have been "hugged" into affairs**. Most affairs of women start because of a lack of affection from the husband.

Ladies, what does affection say to you? In his book, Harley says that when a husband shows affection to his wife, it sends the following messages:

- *"I'll take care of you and protect you. You are important to me, and I don't want anything to happen to you."*

- *"I am concerned about the problems you face, and I am with you."*

- *"I think you have done a good job, and I am so thankful for you."*

For the wife, affection is the **cement** of her relationship with her man. With it, she becomes tightly **bonded** to him. **Men, pay attention. Did you get that point? Nothing is more important.**

Still need some help? Here are some practical suggestions for husbands. Hug and kiss your wife frequently. You can't hug her too many times. Tell her that you love her while you are having breakfast together. Kiss her before you leave for work. Call her during the day to see how she is doing. Bring her flowers once in a while as a surprise, and don't forget the little card to go with it. Each year remember her on her birthday, anniversary, Mother's Day, Valentine's Day, and Christmas. After work, call her before you leave for home so that she knows when to expect you. When you arrive home from work, give her a hug and a kiss and spend a few minutes talking to her about how *her* day went. Help with the dishes after dinner. Find out from her what fulfills her and create a plan for making it a habit in your life. What begins as uncomfortable will soon become second nature to you.

Conversation. Here is a major difference in men and women. Many women will spend hours with each other on the telephone, while men rarely call each other just to chat. Men do better with conversing when they are dating because they are trying to get to know this special little lady. Don't let that stop after marriage!

When a woman talks with her husband, she is bonding with him. Again men, communication with your wife will enable her to meet your needs. To be blunt, talking and sex are connected. Clue. Clue. Clue. Glue. Glue. Glue. You better slow down and take time alone to talk.

As Harley suggests, it's a turnoff when the wife says to her husband, *"Let's talk!"* And he says, *"Sure. What would you like to talk about?"* That's like him saying to her, "Honey, let's make love." And she says, "Why, are you ready to have children?" Just as he finds sex enjoyable in its own right, his wife feels the same about conversation.

When a man returns home from a business trip or an extended time apart from his wife, he will want to bond with her physically, but the wife is going to need to talk. In this way, she is bonding again, too. Let's wise up guys!

Honesty and Openness. A wife must have a husband who is honest and open with her. If he is not, it destroys her **trust and her security.** If she cannot trust him, she has no foundation on which to build a solid relationship. A wife should know her husband better than anyone else in the world—even his parents. This will include knowing his good feelings, bad feelings, frustrations, problems, and fears. The Bible refers to this bond as *"two becoming one"* (Gen. 2:21-25).

Adam and Eve had total transparency in their relationship. Everything was "naked" and open. No shame. No inhibitions. Men sometimes are afraid for a wife to see that they have cracks in their armor. Husbands worry that if our wives see our hurts and fears, they will lose respect. They won't! Wives want to feel that they know you fully. There's no place for secrecy. If my spouse does not have a right to my e-mail account, my phone, my computer, etc., there is a crack in my marriage!!

I love this statement from Willard Harley: *"Whatever advantage a man may gain in being secretive, closed, or even dishonest, he wins it at the expense of his wife's security and marital fulfillment. She must come to find him predictable; a blending of her mind with his should exist so that she can 'read his mind.' When a woman reaches that level of trust, she is able to love her husband more fully."*(pg. 102).

Financial Support. As we studied in the lesson on "Constructing the Husband," a wife wants a husband who is striving to provide to meet the family's needs. Financial stress is a leading cause of divorce, and God has strong words for the lazy man who will not provide for his family (1 Tim. 5:8; Prov. 24:30-

34; 26:13-15). For marriages to be protected from burden, men need to work hard to provide for their families.

On each person's part this effort will mean budgeting, being careful about unnecessary purchases, and avoiding getting into financial debt. A simple rule is to **spend less than you make**. Sounds simple, but it works. Just strive to live comfortably. That's all that is needed: food, clothing, shelter. If we put the kingdom of God first, He promises to provide what we need (Matt. 6:25-34).

What's that oft repeated saying? *"A lot of folks buy things they don't need with money they don't have to impress people they don't like."* Be wary about trying to keep up with the Joneses! If you could be a fly on the wall in the Joneses' house, you might find out that things are not going so well there.

Family commitment. Commitment and spiritual leadership were also discussed in an earlier lesson, but it is important to remember that a godly woman wants a husband who is a spiritual leader (Eph. 5:25-27). God expects him to look after her spiritually and protect her. Adam was held responsible for sin entering the world. He knew better and did not protect Eve or forbid her from doing what was sinful (Rom 5:12). A godly man will "put his foot down" when his wife is flirting with sin.

She also wants a man who looks after the spiritual needs of the children (Eph. 6:4; Dt. 6:5-9). Men are wimping out all over the nation, failing to be men. It is killing this country. When a man pulls up in his driveway at the end of the day, he should pray a prayer for strength, asking God, *"God, be with me now as I enter my home. The greatest work I will do all day is what will be done between these walls tonight with my wife and children."*

Since we have entered the "grey hair" and "grandpa" stage of our lives, we are convinced more than ever that men who leave **great legacies** understand that there are a **few things** in life that must be done, done consistently, and never compromised. Fulfilling the needs of a wife and being her spiritual leader are at the top of the list of those things. Husbands need to remember: *"If your wife is not happy, it might not be your fault, but it is your responsibility."*

THE NEED TO MEET THE NEEDS

What happens when these needs are not met? When is it that most affairs occur? It is when one or both of the partners in a marriage feel that their needs are not being met. We cannot emphasize this enough.

Willard Harley concludes, *"I am all for commitment, and I agree that trust is a vital bonding link in any marriage. But twenty-five years of experience with thousands of people has taught me an undeniable truth:* **If any of a spouse's five basic needs go unmet, that spouse becomes vulnerable to the temptation of an affair."** [9] We are unwise, to say the least, if we ever ignore these things.

Again, beware!

---

[9] Harley, *His Needs, Her Needs.*

QUESTIONS

1. As a Christian, do you agree that the five needs of husbands listed by Harley are really the top five needs?

   - Are these needs in the correct order?

   - Should other things be added?

2. What scriptural reasons can you give to support the idea that a wife should be concerned about providing "recreational companionship" for her husband?

3. Is it important for a wife to try to be physically attractive to her husband? Why?

4. Does the Bible emphasize the need for wives and mothers to have careers or to keep and manage the home? Where does the Bible put its emphasis for the wife and mother (Titus 2:4-5; 1 Tim. 5:14; Prov. 31)?

   If the wife does work outside the home, should the husband feel any extra obligation in helping her keep and manage the house? Why or why not?

5. Why do some husbands become workaholics? What can wives do to help prevent this?

6. What are some specific things husbands need from their wives in the way of respect as they strive to provide for the family?

7. If a husband's needs are not being met, or if his wife for some reason cannot meet his needs, what does God expect of him (1 Cor. 13:5-7)?

8. What might we expect the effect to be on the home when the husband's needs are being met?

9. Are the five needs of wives listed by Harley accurate? Are there other needs that should be included?

10. In 1 Samuel 1:1-8, Elkanah has a conversation with his wife Hannah. Did his conversation meet her needs? Why or why not?

11. What problems could arise in a marriage when husbands and wives hide things from one another and fail to be transparent with each other?

12. Does a wife need a husband who will help her avoid or quit sinning?

13. Do you agree with this charge to husbands: *"If your wife is not happy, it might not be your fault, but it is your responsibility"?*

    If a husband understands that it is his responsibility if his wife is not happy or her needs are not met, what are some of the things he will do?

Chapter 8

Strategies for Solving Conflicts & Divorce-Proofing our Marriages (1)

—•◉•—

Today with such a high percentage of divorces in our land, the devil is surely working to devour our homes (1 Pet. 5:8). Even more marriages are in a state of *emotional divorce*. A couple lives under the same roof, shares the same bed, but the two are complete strangers to each other and often to the children as well. We must dig in our heels and determine to serve the Lord—all the while growing in our marriage (Josh. 24:15).

The dream or ideal state of the home is one that functions exactly as God intended and designed it. This is where we should all strive to be. It's what we felt when we dated and what brought us to the altar to be married. It's not marital perfection. There is no such place. Every marriage needs constant work and maintenance. But it is *real satisfaction* in our relationship!

STAGES OF MARRIAGES IN A DOWNWARD SPIRAL

We appreciate the memorable way in which the downward spiral of marriage has been laid out by Dr. Gary and Barbara Rossberg in their Bible-principled book, *Divorce Proof Your Marriage*. Below is a summary of how they describe this downward spiral in marriage. At the bottom rung, we will speak of why we must not let our marriages crumble.

➤ **DISAPPOINTMENT.** Many marriages are in this state. It happens when you realize you didn't get a perfect mate: a dream partner. The honeymoon ends, and the glow of the first year fades. These disappointments can come from the following:

1. Unmet needs.
2. Irritating habits.
3. Offending or hurting one another, intentionally or not.
4. Collisions of different backgrounds, personalities, and male/female differences.

This disappointment stage is not always a bad place to be as long as we recognize the problems and each spouse determines to work on himself or herself to improve. Some are able to work out of the disappointment stage because they are *teachable*; they learn from their mistakes, and they are willing to admit that what they are doing isn't working. They truly want to be what the Lord wants them to be. This desire drives them. Others are *unteachable;* they allow disappointments to pile up, and they go to the next stop.

➤ **DISCOURAGEMENT.** In this stage of a failing marriage, there is an overwhelming feeling of sadness and frustration that settles in when things do not improve in the relationship. The *women may verbalize* it to other women. The *men often stew* and don't verbalize it. But both may begin to **shrink back** from time together, intimacy, and attempts to resolve conflict. Discouragement leads downward to the next stage.

➤ **DISTANCE.** Here the couple does everything but talk. Have you seen them at restaurants? It's the same way at home. Strangers under the same roof. No excitement in each other. Boredom in the bedroom. This point is where **interests begin in things outside the marriage**, instead of in things that would work to deepen the couple's relationship. The husband may focus on career, sports, hobbies, or projects. The wife allows her life to be taken over by her children, career, volunteer work, or friendships. A couple needs to be together (Gen. 2:18). Otherwise, they are fighting against God's plan. Do not accept this stage!! The dream can be recaptured!!

➢ **DISCONNECT.** God wired us to connect, to care deeply, and to share each other's desires, fears, struggles, and pain. If *discouragement* and *distance* continue long enough, there soon comes no desire to connect. Trust is lost. Intimacy is rare. **Warning!!** The need to connect with another at a deep level is still there. This stage is where affairs occur!!

➢ **DISCORD.** Conflicts, once suppressed, now surface. There are criticisms, arguments, angry outbursts, and wounds. Bitterness rules the day (Col. 3:19; Heb. 12:15). It's like being at war most of the time, and spouses feel as if they are "sleeping with the enemy," if they are sleeping together at all. Some begin to wonder if life would be better without their spouse.

➢ **EMOTIONAL DIVORCE.** The couple is still legally married but separated in heart. The *relationship is dead*. It may be if the couple are Christians, they have a determination not to get a legal divorce. Thank God, His law is at least respected enough to stop them from going to the courthouse. God hates divorce (Mal. 2:16). What He has joined together, man is not to put asunder (Mark 10:9). But is God pleased with us living here in this stage even if we don't legally divorce? Is this what He had in mind? Surely not. Still, all is not lost. God can resurrect a dead marriage and prevent a couple from going to the final stage!

➢ **DIVORCE.** To keep us from ever even using the word "divorce" in our relationships, let us consider the great devastation divorce brings. After a lesson on divorce, Jeff was met at the door by a lady weeping. She said, *"I just can't speak to you right now."* She returned the next night with a card she gave to him. It simply read, *"Thank you, Jeff! Preach it long and loud! Divorce is nothing but a living death! It doesn't get easier. It always hurts bad, but others must know this so that they might not make this mistake. Thanks again."*

Divorce can affect one's self-esteem and even one's health when God's law is broken (Prov. 4:20-22). It creates financial difficulties. It often seems the lawyers are the only ones who prosper. One may have to watch the children grow up only in pictures. It rips away a child's security blanket and often leads to greater instability. Sister Irven Lee used to teach in her classes, *"Children need LSD. Love, Security, and Discipline."* Are any of these things in divorce? Beware of doing things that cause little ones to stumble (Mt. 18:6). The children's future weddings, birthdays, and holidays are often awkward. But most of all, if a couple divorces without scriptural grounds, and then one of them marries another, that person commits adultery. Unless one repents and seeks forgiveness, committing adultery will affect the wellbeing of the soul for all eternity (Mt. 5:32; Gal. 5:19-21). Could anything be worse?

In this lesson, and the next couple of lessons, we will be looking at some strategies and steps for solving conflict; we will be considering truths from God's word that reveal His way of preventing marriages from spiraling down to emotional divorce and show His power for resurrecting marriages that have died.

FIRST STRATEGY: LOVING COMMUNICATION

David Mace, the past president of the American Association of Marriage Counselors, has said that "Poor communication is the main problem in 86% of all troubled marriages." The Bible says that *"Death and life are in the power of the tongue, and those who love it will eat its fruit"* (Prov. 18:21). Truly, the death or life of a marriage relationship is often in the power of the tongue.

God has designed man and woman to become "one" in marriage (Gen. 2:24; Mt. 19). Being "one" does not mean that the man and woman must give up their individual identities, but they must fit their two personalities together to form a single unit—like pieces of a jigsaw puzzle, or the gears of a watch. To accomplish this, they must be willing to share their thoughts and feelings, their dreams, their goals, and their aspirations. But before communication can reach that lofty level, two people must simply learn to communicate about their everyday activities, including the joys and frustrations, plans and accomplishments, hopes and concerns of daily life.

Adam and Eve are a good illustration of transparency in marriage. It was only when sin entered that they started hiding and blaming one another and others. Before sin entered, everything was so transparent and open. Much is said in the words, *"And they were both naked, the man and his wife and were not ashamed"* (Gen. 2:25). Everything was naked and laid open. Since there was no sin, there was nothing to hide. Since there were no other people, there were no unwise comparisons. Since they were comfortable with their nakedness, there were no sexual inhibitions and no shame. In every sense of the word, they demonstrated what it means to "know" one another (Gen. 4:1). Marriages need this transparency.

The Hebrew word for "know" is *yada.* In marriage, we need lots of this kind of yada, yada, yada. This openness may be harder for husbands than for wives, but the rewards of transparency are abundant. One husband says, *"I felt such a need to be respected for my strength. I was afraid to let the cracks in my armor show to my wife. I was afraid she would lose respect for me. I would not let her see my hurts or my fears. I knew I needed to be more transparent, and I slowly tried to let my wife see all. I found that instead of not respecting me, her love grew deeper for me. We have become close beyond my wildest imaginations, and I am happy to seek the refuge of her care."*

What good communication requires from the communicator:

- **Self-revelation.** You cannot expect another person to know what is in your heart and head without making an effort to communicate it. Your spouse is not a mind reader. No one can know what is going on inside another person's head unless that person communicates or reveals it in some way (1 Cor. 2:11).

  Self-revelation also involves the confession of faults, which we will discuss in the next lesson on *forgiveness*. Good things happen in a relationship when two people are transparent with their shortcomings and faults (James 5:16).

- **Think before speaking.** Hasty words invariably create problems for the person who speaks them (Prov. 29:20). Guarding what comes out of your mouth will prevent many problems in your marriage (Prov. 21:23).

- **A clear message**. Read 1 Corinthians 14:8-9. This text contains specific guidance for speaking in the church, but the truth it contains may be applied generally. What happens if the trumpet does not give a clear sound? People who hear don't understand the message! If you speak, but the person you are speaking to does not understand, it is like you are just speaking into the air!

- **Mean what you say; say what you mean.** James 5:12 says, *"But let your 'Yes' be 'Yes,' and your 'No,' 'No,' lest you fall into judgment."* The apostle Paul said the same (2 Cor. 1:17-18). It was Jesus who led the way in this message (Mt. 5:37). What happens when you tell someone "yes," but you really mean "no"? The person who receives the message acts one way, when you really want them to act another. Frustration ensues! Have you been guilty of this kind of miscommunication with your spouse? Can you see that sending these false signals is undermining your marriage?

- **Check to see if you are getting through.** In Matthew 13:51, after communicating several parables to His disciples, Jesus asks, *"Have you understood all these things?"* Jesus was the greatest communicator to ever live on earth. If He felt the need to make sure He was getting through, it would surely be wise for us to do the same when talking with those we love.

What good communication requires from the listener:

- **Being quick to listen, slow to speak, and slow to wrath** (James 1:19). Do you understand the difference between being quick to speak and quick to listen? The first is done with the mouth open, and the second is done with the mouth closed! Make sure that you hear out the other person thoroughly before responding. They may not be saying what you thought they were going to say. The Bible says that *"He who answers a matter before he hears it, it is folly and shame to him"* (Prov. 18:13).

- **An open heart**. In 2 Corinthians 6:11-13 the Apostle Paul expresses concern that he wasn't connecting in his communication with the Corinthians because their hearts were not open to him or his words. He writes, *"O Corinthians! We have spoken openly to you, our heart is wide open. You are not restricted by us, but you are restricted by your own affections. Now in return for the same (I speak as to children), you also be open."* We must speak and hear with wide-open hearts if communication is to be effective. The Corinthians needed to open themselves up to Paul. Their sinful ways, their pride, and their stubbornness made it hard for Paul to communicate with them.

In later lessons we will study methods for opening closed hearts, including such things as how to express love appropriately, how to seek forgiveness, and how to manage anger.

QUESTIONS

1. List the stages of marriage in the downward spiral to emotional divorce.

2. Give examples of each of the following that might lead to disappointment in a marriage:

    - Irritating habits.

    - Offending or hurting one another, intentionally or not.

    - Collisions of different backgrounds, personalities, and male/female differences.

3. What are some devastating effects of divorce of which you are aware?

4. What percentage of troubled marriages suffer from poor communication between husband and wife?

    - Do you believe that the power of the tongue can kill a marriage?

5. Explain what is involved in "self-revelation" and "transparency."

    • Will a person who practices these things have a "secret self" that his or her spouse is unaware of?

    • In what ways do Adam and Eve demonstrate transparency in their marriage? Did things change after sin entered the picture? If so, how?

6. Think of an instance in your life when you did not communicate clearly and were misunderstood. What problems did that create?

7. Have you been guilty of saying "yes" or "ok" when you really wanted to say "no" or "no way"? What was the result?

8. List examples of things you can say or do to make sure that your words are getting through to the other person.

9. Can you think of a time when you were guilty of responding to someone before hearing him or her out? What was the result?

10. If a person with an open heart tries to communicate to a person with a closed heart, what is usually the result?

Chapter 9

Strategies for Solving Conflicts & Divorce-Proofing our Marriages (2)

If couples really want to have successful, Christlike marriages, they simply must go to the foot of the cross and watch what they see there from the world's greatest husband. He loves His bride with a passion like the world has not seen since.

Think of it. Every attitude and action needed in the home, or all of life for that matter, is seen at the cross of Jesus Christ. Need a simple "How-to Guidebook"? Take what you see there and just do it. This is why the Ephesians 5 instructions use the words "just as" and "as also." We need to do it "just as" Jesus did. And two prominent things we can't miss at the cross are **forgiving love and serving love**.

SECOND STRATEGY: FORGIVING LOVE

It has been said that *"A happy marriage is the union of two good forgivers"* (Robert Quillen). On the other hand, nearly every miserable marriage or rotten relationship is characterized by holding on to grudges, keeping account of wrongs, and wallowing in bitterness. Many in these kinds of relationships do not even understand what forgiveness is, let alone why it is so important, or how to go about giving and receiving it.

Learning to forgive is vital to developing any good relationship. Those who refuse to cultivate this ability are only hurting themselves. Marriage counselor Michele Weiner-Davis makes the following observations on this point:

> *Lack of forgiveness imprisons you. It takes its toll on your physical and emotional health. It keeps you stuck in the deepest of relationship ruts. No matter how justified you feel about your point of view regarding your partner's insensitive behavior, you still are miserable. When you wake up each morning, a gray tint shadows your life. You walk around with a low-grade depression. You can't feel joy because you're too busy being angry or feeling disappointed. In the face of these fairly obvious disadvantages, you hang on to your belief that, since you feel let down, you must not give in....*
>
> *Letting go of resentment can set you free. It can bring more love and happiness into your life. It opens the door to intimacy and connection. It makes you feel whole. Forgiving others takes strength, particularly when you feel wronged, but the fortitude required to forgive pales in comparison to the energy necessary to maintain a sizable grudge. The person most hurt by holding out or blaming is YOU, no matter what the circumstances.*[10]

Whether deliberately or not, people in close relationships will inevitably hurt each other. But regardless of who did what, *every offense* can have a positive resolution. However, this can't happen when offenses and hurts are ignored or swept under the carpet. It can't happen until we learn both to seek forgiveness for ourselves and extend forgiveness to others.

WHAT FORGIVENESS IS NOT

Real forgiveness cannot occur if we are walking around with a false concept of what forgiveness actually is. Clarity on this point

---

[10] Michele Weiner-Davis, "Forgiveness is a Gift You Give Yourself," http://divorcebusting.com, (2009).

is crucial to constructing good relationships.

- **Forgiveness is not *just* forgetting something**. It is not sweeping something under the carpet, burying it, or pretending that it didn't happen. If you cover the weeds in your garden, they are still there. If you just cut them, they are still there and will probably grow back. Real forgiveness is tearing the weeds out by the roots, so the garden will flourish.

  There is a bit of a gender problem to overcome when it comes to understanding this aspect of forgiveness. Men tend to gloss over their sins without saying "I'm sorry." Women generally operate differently. When the man says, "Just drop it," she will still think that secretly he is not sorry for what he has done, and the matter will remain unresolved. She has to clear the air. Women have an easier time saying "I'm sorry" because it signals **love** when she says it. Men are afraid to say "I'm sorry" because they fear losing **respect**. Many men *feel* weak when they apologize, but the reality is that *seeking forgiveness shows great strength.*

- **Forgiveness is not excusing something**, or saying whatever was done is "Okay." We forgive people of things that are not okay. When we excuse people, we don't need to forgive them. We excuse people when we understand that they are not to blame. We have to forgive people when they *are* to blame.

- **Forgiveness is not tolerance**. Tolerance is enduring something hard, painful, or irritating. A lot of tolerance, longsuffering, and forbearance is necessary in any healthy relationship, but it should not be confused with forgiveness.

- **Forgiveness is not acceptance**. You may accept things about a person that you do not particularly like. This is needed in a good relationship. But forgiveness assumes that someone has been wronged or mistreated.[11]

WHAT FORGIVENESS INVOLVES

If we are to learn how to forgive and how to seek forgiveness, we must learn from the Lord. He is in the forgiveness business! *He has left us a pattern for forgiving and being forgiven.* We are to forgive like He forgives (Eph. 4:32; Col. 3:13)! Did you notice the "just as" and "even as" words in those passages?

God's process for forgiveness involves the following steps:

- **The guilty must recognize and repent of their sins** (Acts 3:19; 8:22). We are not encouraging the guilty to repent of their sins by pretending they didn't happen, excusing them, tolerating them, or accepting them. The Lord's way is to *lovingly rebuke* the sinner (Rev. 3:19). That is the approach He tells us to use as well. In Luke 17:3, Jesus said, *"If your brother sins against you, rebuke him; and if he repents, forgive him."*

- **The guilty must confess their sins.** God's forgiveness is conditioned on confession (1 John 1:9). Even so, He expects us to confess our sins to one another so that we can forgive each other and healing can occur (James 5:16). Confession involves an *open acknowledgment* of a particular transgression (Psalm 32:5).

- **The forgiver must erase the transgression.** God forgives us thoroughly. Aren't you glad He does? Psalm 103:12 states that *"As far as the east is from the west, so far has He removed our transgressions from us."* The Lord does not "remember" the sins and lawless deeds of those He has forgiven (Heb. 10:17; Isa. 43:25). Once we have forgiven another, the matter is erased from the

---

[11] Adapted from Gary Chapman, *The Marriage You've Always Wanted Bible Study*, (Chicago: Moody, 2009) 25.

record. It will not be brought up again to win an argument, to belittle, or to disparage.

Keys to seeking to forgive and be forgiven

Two important characteristics that will smooth out this process of forgiveness are **humility** and **self-awareness**. It all works so much more efficiently when we are aware of our faults and the effect they have on others, and when we have the humility to admit those faults and seek reconciliation. If you are aware that a loved one has something against you for something you have done, go to them and seek reconciliation (Matt. 5:23-24). On the other hand, if a loved one sins against you, make them aware of it and give them a chance to make it right (Matt. 18:15)

THIRD STRATEGY: SERVING LOVE

Most young, unmarried people imagine marriage to be a relationship in which they will have their own needs fulfilled. A young man wants a wife who will satisfy his sexual desires, build his ego, and provide for his comfort. A young lady wants a man who will show her affection, give her security, and be a caring father to her children. Newlyweds who are entirely focused on their own wants will rapidly become disillusioned with marriage. When BOTH spouses are focused on having their OWN NEEDS fulfilled, it is certain that NEITHER will be satisfied for long. The same dynamic is often at work in relationships between friends, siblings, and coworkers, and it always makes for a very unfulfilling human connection.

Seeking Self or Losing Self?

Our culture tends to train us for assertive selfishness, not humble service. In contrast, the concepts of selflessness and sacrifice are fundamental to Christianity. To be followers of Christ, we must deny ourselves (Luke 9:23-24). This mindset should have been in us when we took up our cross to follow Him, crucified self, and then were buried with Him in baptism (Mt. 16:24-25; Rom. 6:6; Gal 5:24). Our old selfish ways are to be killed. It has been well pointed out that in the first century a criminal might walk by with his cross, but you never see him come back. The cross finishes the old man and his sinful patterns. So, we have to make a choice. Will we seek ourselves or lose ourselves?

According to James 3:14-15, the origin of self-seeking is earthly and demonic. It comes straight from hell. It creates confusion and evil in relationships. To be blunt, when we are self-seeking, we are allowing the devil to control our lives and our relationships. He is our father in those moments (John 8:44a). The self-seeking person is hollow, unreliable, faithless, and useless (Jude 12-13). By focusing only on himself, he spoils every human relationship and ruins himself for eternity.

In previous lessons, we have studied extensively the roles of husbands and wives, emphasizing the duty of each spouse to meet the other's needs. Husbands and wives must see themselves as *servants* to one another. Disciples like Peter and Paul called themselves "slaves" in the opening words of their letters (2 Peter 1:1; Rom. 1:1). To be a slave is to have no rights of one's own. Each spouse needs to quit talking about "my rights" and start focusing on "my responsibilities."

Jesus calls us to be servants in marriage, just as He was to His followers (John 13:1-17; Eph. 5:25; 1 Peter 3:7). It's not a 50/50 arrangement. Each spouse must give 100% to serving God and each other – just as Christ did (Phil. 2:3-8). There must be a resolve to meet each other's needs totally. Strive to make it so that your spouse feels that he or she is married to someone with the character and qualities of Christ Himself.

Love motivates us to seek forgiveness and to serve (Luke 7:47; Gal. 5:13-15). The absence of these qualities is a sure indication that love is lacking, and the home is in danger of collapse.

QUESTIONS

1. What is the difference between forgiveness and each of the following?

   - Forgetting

   - Tolerating

   - Excusing

   - Accepting

2. What is involved in forgiving someone the way Christ forgives us?

   - What steps should be taken by a person seeking forgiveness?

   - Once these steps have been taken, what should be the response from the person who has been sinned against?

3. Do the Scriptural patterns for forgiving and seeking forgiveness apply to relationships between spouses? Other family members? Friends?

   - Do these patterns apply all the time? Explain.

   - Are there exceptions? If so, what are they?

4. What would you say to a person who says, "I have forgiven him or her, but I still have bad feelings when I remember what he or she did"?

5. What are we to do with "all" of our bitterness (Eph. 4:31) ?

6. Is it a sin for a husband to be bitter toward his wife (Col. 3:19)? Why or why not?

7. Homework: Practice seeking forgiveness. Read Job 13:23. Put this prayer in your own words and ask God to show you where you have sinned against others (parents, siblings, spouse, friends, or other family members).

   - As things come to mind, write them down. Make a list.
   - Confess these failures to God and ask for forgiveness and strength.
   - At an appropriate time, share this list with the one(s) you've sinned against and ask for forgiveness from them.

8. How does the principle of self-denial apply to the marriage relationship? If we truly died to self the day we were baptized, how will that impact our marriage?

9. What metaphors are used in Jude 12-13 to illustrate the character of those who serve only themselves? Explain how these metaphors illustrate self-seeking.

10. How will "going to the cross" each day make a difference in our homes?

Chapter 10

Strategies for Solving Conflicts & Divorce-Proofing our Marriages (3)

━━━━━━━━━━━━━━━●━━━━━━━━━━━━━━━

THE FOURTH STRATEGY:
THE ACHIEVEMENT OF AGREEMENT

Union with Unity

If you tie the tails of two cats together, you have made a union, but it is doubtful that you will have created unity. The union of two human beings in a relationship does not guarantee unity either. Unless there is mutual agreement on goals and the appropriate actions to achieve those goals, the best that can be hoped for is an unsatisfying and unpleasant coexistence. The achievement of agreement is critical to the success of most human relationships, especially marriage. Long ago the prophet Amos rhetorically asked, *"Can two walk together, unless they are agreed?"* (Amos 3:3).

The Divine Model

God the Father and His Son Jesus Christ provide the perfect pattern of unity in a relationship. We see them working together in Creation (Gen. 1:26). We learn that the Son always submitted to the will of the Father (John 8:29). We observe that, while the Son submitted, He felt completely free to express His own feelings (Matt. 26:39, 42). In all of these passages, the Father and the Son are *one!* They each fill a different role. The Father purposes and directs, and the Son lovingly and humbly submits (Phil. 2:5-9). The result is single-minded agreement!

The unity between the Father and the Son illustrates that understanding your role in a relationship is vital to unity in that relationship. In any endeavor requiring people to work together towards common ends, there must be an understanding of the role each person is to play. A football team can't function if everybody is playing quarterback! Achieving agreement in marriage requires that each person know his or her role. In our lessons on the roles of husbands and wives, we emphasized that the man is to be the *head* and *leader* in the home, and the wife is to be the *submissive helper*. When each person stays focused on fulfilling his or her role in the relationship, unity is easily achievable.

The Importance of Truth in Achieving Agreement

Real agreement can never be achieved if both parties are not being completely truthful. Lack of candor or deceit by one person produces agreement, but the agreement is fraudulent! Unity in spiritual matters is based on truth (Eph. 4:15-16). Ephesians 4:25 commands Christians to put away lying and *"let each one of you speak truth with his neighbor, for we are members of one another."* Note that truthfulness is demanded because of the relationship we have with one another as *members* of *one body.*

Unity in any family relationship must be based on truth. When we shade the truth, flatter, or lie to spare feelings, we are destroying relationships (Prov. 26:28). We must speak truthfully—say what we mean and mean what we say (James 5:12). Often in a marriage, one or both partners will claim they "don't care" about a given matter when they really *do care.* For couples who have problems honestly communicating their level of concern about a given issue, counselors suggest that couples ask each other to rate the intensity of their feelings about a matter from 0 to 10. Rating helps clarify and communicate to the other spouse a truer picture so there can be *real* mutual agreement when unity is achieved.

It has been observed that there are basically three ways for two people in a relationship to reach successful agreement:

- **Meet you in the middle:** Voluntary compromise somewhere in the middle of two differing positions.

- **Meet you on your side**: One person gives up his or her original position in favor of the other, either because they see that it is a better choice or in order to put the other person's needs first.

- **Meet you later:** Immediate agreement cannot easily be reached, but it is recognized that with time for reflection, gathering more information, and even physical rest, agreement is possible.[12]

Different situations require different approaches to reaching agreement. Couples that dwell together in unity have the wisdom to know when to apply the most appropriate of these three approaches.

THE FIFTH STRATEGY: ANGER MANAGEMENT

Anger isn't necessarily a bad thing. It is like pain in the body or smoke from a fire; it warns us that something significant is happening that needs to be dealt with. A high percentage of married couples will never realize this, and so their marriages suffer needlessly. Relationship expert, Gary Chapman, writes: "Couples typically deal with anger in one of two ways. They either explode and express their anger in violent and destructive behavior, or they hold it inside and allow it to burn and smolder…neither of these ways is biblical." The Bible way is to take charge of our spirits and learn to control the flow of our anger (Prov. 16:32).

---

[12] Adapted from Gary Chapman, *The Marriage You've Always Wanted*, (Chicago: Moody, 2009), 78-79.

In a healthy relationship, both partners are like smoke detectors. Think about it. A smoke alarm detects the presence of smoke and warns us that there is a fire. When we are alerted that fire is present, we can then either fight the fire or escape it. Anger is like smoke. It's not the source of relationship and personal problems, but it warns us that they are there. We can use anger to detect where the fundamental problems are. That is not to say that anger is not dangerous on its own. Anger, like smoke, can destroy a person or a family who never even feels the heat of the flames that cause it. Anger that is not understood, dealt with, and managed can prevent the development of every positive relationship process that we have studied to this point— communication, forgiveness, service, and achieving agreement.

Divine Anger

The emotion of anger is not sinful in itself. Jesus felt and expressed anger as He lived as a man on earth (Mark 3:1-5). *"God is angry with the wicked every day"* (Ps. 7:11). He is even angry with His children at times (Josh. 7:1; Heb. 3:10). But God is slow to become angry, and when He does, it usually doesn't last long – only "for a moment" (Ps. 103:8; 30:5). His anger is always righteous because He is always righteous (Ps. 119:137). God's anger has a purpose. It is not selfish or impure. It often expresses displeasure with sin and helps sinners see their urgent need to repent!

The Wrath of Man

Human anger is typically not nearly as purely motivated or righteously directed as the anger of God. For instance, in the story of the prodigal son, the older brother's anger was caused by jealousy and self-righteousness (Luke 15:28-30). Cain's anger in Genesis 4:5 was motivated by his own failure when compared to his brother's righteousness (1 John 3:12). In these cases, and many more that could be cited, we see what James means when he says that *"the wrath of man does not produce the righteousness of God"* (James 1:20).

The book of Proverbs contains a lot of wisdom about controlling anger. It teaches that a quick-tempered man acts foolishly and exalts folly (Prov. 14:17, 29). What a blessing it would be if each person in the home could understand the truth of that! It is the fool who "vents all his feelings" (Prov. 29:11). If you would call to mind the top five most regrettable, foolish, and embarrassing things that you have ever said or done, you would likely realize that most of them were done in anger!

A furious man abounds in transgression (Prov. 29:22). Wrath and anger keep him from being kind, tenderhearted, and forgiving (Eph. 4:31). ***Unresolved or mismanaged anger gives a place to the devil in your home*** (Eph. 4:26-27). If he is allowed to stay, he will ruin things for sure. Couples must learn how to manage anger constructively. Here is the Biblical approach to doing just that:

If you are angry...

- **Admit it.** Tell the truth! (Eph. 4:25)
- **Restrain your words.** Do not say everything that comes to your mind (Prov. 10:19; 29:11)!
- **Share your problem.** Explain why you are angry. Talk about what you *feel* and *why*. It may help to take a time-out and collect your thoughts first.
- **Look for a solution.** Ask your partner for help! Focus on what *you can do* more than what your partner can do to alleviate the cause of your anger. [13]

If your partner is angry...

- **Answer softly.** A soft answer turns away wrath. (Prov. 15:1)
- **Look beyond being personally offended** or attempting to defend yourself to helping your partner deal constructively with his or her problem. Remember that love *"does not behave rudely, does not seek its own, is not provoked, thinks no evil"* (1 Cor. 13:5).

---

[13] Adapted from Chapman, *The Marriage You've Always Wanted,* 89.

Sadly, the two most common ways of dealing with anger in a typical marriage relationship are *blowing up* or *clamming up*. Both of these approaches violate the Scriptures we have studied. That means *they are sinful!!!* We need to repent and confess if we have been guilty of handling anger in these sinful ways (1 John 1:9).

There is a big difference between controlling anger and suppressing anger. It is neither Scriptural nor good for us to simply refuse to allow ourselves to be angry (Eph. 4:26). The Scriptures do not counsel us to suppress anger, but to put it off (Col. 3:8; Eph. 4:31). This *can be done* by using the Biblical approach to managing anger that we've outlined above.

QUESTIONS

1. What is necessary for two to walk together? (Amos 3:3)

2. What important lessons can we learn from the way God the Father and His Son Jesus model achieving unity?

3. Based on Ephesians 4:15-16 & 25, do you agree with this statement: *Truth results in unity, and unity results in truth?* Explain.

4. Give some examples of how dishonesty fosters division in a family.

5. What are the three basic ways for reaching an agreement between two parties in a marriage?

   How can you know which method should be used in a given situation?

6. How is anger like smoke?

7. What causes God to be angry, and what purposes are served by Him expressing His anger?

   Does God's anger come from selfish or impure motives? Does it cause Him to sin?

8. What caused Cain to be angry?

   What caused the older brother in the story of the prodigal son to be angry?

   What were the consequences of their anger on their family relationships?

9. What should you do if you have been guilty of handling anger either by *clamming up* or *blowing up?*

10. **Homework:** Write down these steps for dealing with anger on a piece of paper and keep it with you this week. When you realize you are getting angry, look at the steps and practice them. Take note of the effect this has on your relationships at home, at work, or with friends.

    If you are angry...

    - **Admit it.** Tell the truth!
    - **Restrain your words.** Do not say everything that comes to your mind!
    - **Share your problem.** Explain why you are angry. Talk about what you *feel* and *why*. It may help to take a time-out and collect your thoughts first.
    - **Look for a solution.** Ask the person you are angry with for help! Focus on what *you can do* more than what they can do to alleviate the cause of your anger.

Chapter 11

Avoiding Home-Wreckers

*"Don't ruin other people's happiness
just because you can't find your own."*

*"Home-wreckers wouldn't have a home to wreck if someone had
not let them in the front door."*

*"I set my GPS to 'home-wrecker,'
and I ended up in your driveway."*

*"If you manage to steal my man, steal my shoes too, cuz eventually
you'll be walking in them!"*

*"At the end of the day...just remember: Home-wreckers can't
wreck a home by themselves."*

All of the above are quotes about home-wreckers easily found
on the internet. A quick Google search revealed that folks are
steaming mad about home wreckers. Some of those home-
wreckers even have their names plastered on cyberspace walls for
all the world to see. They destroy the security God meant for
every home to offer spouses and children. And as we shall see in
this lesson, home-wreckers come in many forms.

For a woman in particular, security is extremely important.
She needs a secure foundation on which to build a family and a

home. None of that comes quickly or immediately. It takes time to build. But while the foundations are being laid, it is easy to damage a relationship. The solving of problems should not be put off. They need to be handled before they can cause lasting harm.

The Bible says it this way: *"Catch us the foxes, the little foxes that spoil the vines, for our vines have tender grapes"* (Song of Solomon 2:15). As couples, the vines are our lives, and the fruitage is our developing love. Catch the foxes! Take care of those little problems before they ruin your lives! It is so easy for young couples to ignore caution and allow impulsiveness and immaturity to guide them. We must learn to see potential risks and choose to avoid things that may cause lasting harm.

HABITS FROM THE SINGLE LIFE

Those periods in our lives when we make major changes are always difficult. We form habits at certain stages of our lives which are appropriate at the time, but which may not work well at the next stage. Those same habits, which were harmless or helpful earlier in life, can cause difficulty later. For instance, it is appropriate for children and teens to spend large amounts of time playing and engaging in other activities that need to be curtailed as adults. There comes a time to put away childish things (1 Cor. 13:11). Marriage is for adults.

Before marriage, the attention of young men and women is directed toward searching for a mate. Nearly every person you meet of the opposite gender at this stage of life is weighed as to whether or not they are a potential spouse. You do a lot of looking and comparing. But that looking and comparing must end once married. The problem is that the habits of the single life can be hard to break, and it can cause harm in a new marriage.

Early in a marriage, a spouse may not know just how fully he or she can trust the other person—there simply is not enough experience with each other to fall back on. A track record has not been established. The desire to trust is there, but both partners need assurance and reassurance. What will be understood as a harmless look, gesture, or compliment to another person after twenty-five *years* of marriage, may not be perceived that way after 25 *weeks* of marriage. Trust is a foundation in a loving relationship, but trust is something earned when a person demonstrates over and over again that he or she is trustworthy.

When the apostle Paul had the churches send relief funds to the needy saints in Judea, he insisted that each congregation select someone to carry the funds. It wasn't that Paul was not trustworthy; he just didn't want to leave any doubt that everything was aboveboard (2 Cor. 8:18-21). In the same way, even if you and your spouse believe that the other is trustworthy, you need to reinforce that trust with behavior that is always unquestionable. The little things you do out of habit without even thinking about them are going to be noticed.

So, for many newlyweds who are working to build trust, the time has arrived to break old habits and establish new ones. This is particularly true when it comes to habitual ways of interacting with or looking at the opposite sex. A commitment needs to be made such as the one Job made: *"I have made a covenant with my eyes; why then should I look upon a young woman?"* (Job 31:1). Making such a covenant with your eyes will not only help build trust with your spouse, it will also serve to all but eliminate a major source of temptation in your life.

The Bible instructs husbands to be "enraptured" with the love of their wives (Prov. 5:19). A husband who is enraptured with his wife won't be able to keep his eyes off of her. He'll glance at her across a crowded room. He'll let her see the smile on his lips when he makes eye contact with her. When being introduced to someone new, he'll want to include his wife as part of the introductions. These are good habits. And although they are just small things and little gestures, they tell the wife and the world who is important in the man's life.

HOME-WRECKING TEMPTATIONS

Water runs the course of least resistance, and many people navigate their lives in a similar manner. It's the reason that both rivers and people wind up crooked. Satan plays on our basic desires, including the desire for an easy solution. He tempts us with solutions that only temporarily relieve a burden or fulfill a need, but ultimately the devil's easy way results in deep difficulties. Downhill slopes are always easier to travel. You can glide! It's not surprising then that the path to hell is easier to walk than the path to heaven (Matt. 7:13-14).

That brings us to an important discussion of the disastrous consequences of pursuing forbidden experiences, together or separately. Sin can be pleasurable and exciting (Heb. 11:25b). Like a roller coaster, sin is fun because you appear to be defying certain harm—you do something you know is wrong and appear to get away with it (Prov. 9:17). When a marriage becomes stale, there is a temptation to liven things up by seeking the thrill of doing something forbidden (Rom. 7:11). This can lead to married individuals committing a variety of sins. Forbidden experiences that married couples might seek together or separately include pornography, alcohol, drugs, and extramarital sexual relations.

Pornography

Lust is defined as a very strong desire for something that is unlawful to have. Jesus condemned looking at women to lust (Matt. 5:28). If just looking was a problem, then we all would need to wear blinders because we live in a world full of people. But when a guy looks at a girl in order to lust, he commits adultery in his heart. The same would be true of a woman looking at a man to lust. Yes, women can do it too.

We remember the old Coke commercial where the women in a high-rise office building are walking around saying to each other, "Diet Coke break. Diet Coke break." It's not *their* break they are looking forward to. They all gather at the window to look at a construction worker down below. His shirt is off, and his body is muscled and glistening with perspiration. They love watching him take *his* Coke break and plan to meet there each day! Like Potiphar's wife, here is surely an example of a woman having lustful eyes (Gen. 39:6-7).

Looking at pornography is intentionally looking to lust. We live in a world that is technically so advanced that pornography can be delivered to you instantaneously virtually anywhere via television, computer, or cell phone. Millions and millions of people engage in this sin, and many are addicted to it—including an astonishing number of Christians.

In his book, *Finally Free,* author Heath Lambert examines from a biblical perspective what it takes for a Christian to break free from the enslaving and destructive habit of viewing pornography. Here is an overview of some of his findings:

- **God's grace** is the foundation in the fight against pornography. God's grace is powerful; it overtakes and overpowers every sin (Rom. 5:20b-21).
- Christians have access to God's *forgiving and transforming grace* through **repentance** and **confession** (1 John 1:8-9).
- Grace transforms us as we accept God's forgiveness and continually ask for help to overcome, instead of continually wallowing in guilt and self-recrimination (Heb. 4:16). Sorrow for sin is needed, but it must be the godly sorrow that leads to true repentance, not the self-loathing sorrow that leads to death (2 Cor. 7:10; 2:7b).

Specific behaviors for dealing with pornography addiction include the following:

- Seek help from godly, mature Christians (Gal. 6:1-2). *Make yourself accountable* to them for your behavior. Seek help in a timely manner, not after long periods of engaging in sin. The devil loves secrecy. Bringing your sin out from under cover is a major step toward victory.

- Use radical measures to rid yourself from temptation (Matt. 5:27-30).
- Confess your sin to those who are affected by it (Prov. 28:13; James 5:16).
- Use your spouse, or your potential spouse, to fight against pornography.

   Lambert writes, *"You can never stop thinking about something by trying not to think about it. If you want to get something out of your mind, you must think about something else"* (p. 91). Starve your eyes. Bounce your eyes away from every person, billboard, magazine, newspaper ad, etc., that is immodest and sexually provocative. This eye starvation will create a hunger for the one God wants you to hunger for...your spouse. Daydream about her. Don't just empty out evil fantasies. Fill up with the love of your spouse. It's an intoxication God allows (Prov. 5:19). Jesus Himself also taught this empty out and then fill up principle (Luke 11:24-26)

   Like the evil temptress described in Proverbs 5:1-13, the woman featured in pornography is herself lost and in need of direction (5:5-6). She will ruin your life. Focus instead on the wife God has intended for you to have in marriage and on the pure, undefiled satisfaction she provides (Prov. 5:14-23).

- Learn humility. Viewing pornography is selfish and arrogant; it is an "evil thing" that results from being "self-seeking" (James 3:13-16).[14]

Alcohol and drugs

"When a person is under the influence of alcohol, or some other drug, other problems no longer seem significant. The drug deadens the pain and makes it easy to make-believe that nothing is the matter. The only problem is that the problems don't go away." They are still there when you come down from your drug-induced euphoria. In fact, drugs add more problems to your life. See the

---

[14] Heath Lambert, *Finally Free* (Zondervan, 2013).

description of the alcohol abuser in Proverbs 23:29-35! Alcohol deceives the user into thinking the problems go away (Prov. 20:1). But don't let it fool you! It's nothing but a bottled home-wrecker![15]

Serious character flaws and spiritual shortcomings typically develop with the use of alcohol (Isa. 5:11-12, 21-23). Alcohol is a contributing factor in the vast majority of cases of domestic violence and spousal abuse. Studies have shown that there is a direct correlation between the amount a married person drinks and the likelihood that they will get a divorce.[16] Christians are commanded to give up a lifestyle of recreational drinking precisely because it ruins lives in dissipation (1 Peter 4:3-4).

Extramarital relations = Giving up on your spouse!

At times couples may be tempted to give up on their marriage relationship when problems arise. Remember that love *"bears all things, believes all things, hopes all things, endures all things"* (1 Cor. 13:7). Instead of taking the approach of love, many young couples wallow in self-pity and seek sympathy from others when problems arise. They may be heard to whine, *"My husband doesn't understand me; he never listens!"* or, *"My wife never shows me any real affection; I can't even talk to her anymore."* Before you know it, the husband or wife is seeking comfort in the arms of another person.

No amount of rationalization can change the fact that this is adultery, and that anyone who commits it will be judged (Heb. 13:4). Instead of seeking an easy way out of your problem, honor your commitment to your union (Mal. 2:15). Fight for your marriage! Work hard to make the marriage better! It's not the easy

---

[15] The quote in this paragraph and other portions of this section of the lesson are adapted from excellent material by Jeffrey Hamilton, *Preparations for a Lifetime: Temptations*, via http://lavistachurchofchrist.org/LVstudies/Preparation/Temptations.htm

[16] M. Fe Caces, Thomas C. Harford, Gerald D. Williams, and Eleanor Z. Hanna "Alcohol Consumption and Divorce Rates in the United States," *Journal of Studies on Alcohol & Drugs*, Volume 60, Issue 5: September 1999.

way, but it is what is best and what is right! "Tackle the problems in your relationship and work for true solutions, not easy escapes."[17]

---

17 Hamilton, *Preparations for a Lifetime: Temptations*

QUESTIONS

1. What happens if you don't "catch the little foxes" that spoil the tender vines?

2. What are some things that are fine activities for children but need to be curtailed as adults (1 Cor. 13:11)?

3. What can husbands and wives do to build trust and reassure one another of their mutual devotion? What should they avoid doing?

4. Why do rivers and people wind up crooked?

5. How does a Christian access God's grace and forgiveness to overcome the sin of pornography?

6. There is a difference between godly sorrow and the sorrow of the world (2 Cor. 9:10). Give some examples of things that someone might say to himself when he is experiencing the *sorrow of the world* for committing the sin of viewing pornography.

   Give some examples of things that someone might say to himself when he is experiencing *godly sorrow*.

7. What are some radical measures Christians might need to take to rid themselves of the sin of pornography? Consider ways they might need to change things both inside and out.

8. In Proverbs 5, how is a young man instructed to deal with the temptation of an evil woman? How do these instructions translate into dealing with pornography?

9. What is the correlation between drinking alcohol and divorce?

   Why do you think this correlation exists? Explain.

10. Is there any situation or degree of dissatisfaction in a marriage that justifies adultery?

    What must a person do who is living in a state of emotional divorce but desires to repent?

Chapter 12

Building Those New Additions (Children)

●

Quite often when a husband and wife have spent meaningful time alone together in their home, they decide to add on a new addition to the house. Walls may be torn out to enlarge rooms or add on new living spaces. Likewise, the time comes when couples decide they are ready for new additions to their family. They are ready for children.

CHILDREN: THE BLESSING & THE CHALLENGE

Children are a blessing from the Lord and a great source of happiness. Psalm 127:3-5 compares them to arrows and says, *"Happy is the man whose quiver is full of them."* Every parent should appreciate these little gifts from God and prize the reward. One day, down the road, aged parents may enter great battles with their health or other issues and need some help. How nice it is when they reach to their quiver and there's another arrow. What a blessing when children show up to *"repay their parents"* (1 Tim. 5:4)!

But know this—while children bring great joy into a family, they are also a source of concern. At times it can escalate to all-out anxiety and distress. It is the toughest job on the planet and a grave responsibility. Someone has said, *"If bringing up children was easy, it would not start with something called LABOR."*

God gives parents the duty of bringing up children with the very highest standards— *"in the training and admonition of the Lord"* (Eph. 6:4). If children are like arrows in the hand of a warrior (Psalm 127:4), they must be crafted to fly straight and true!

Think soberly about this. Before conception, children are nonexistent. Once conceived, they will spend eternity *somewhere.* That "somewhere" will depend largely on the training given by their parents. *Prospective parents should feel the weight of that!*

Most parents feel ill-equipped for this tremendous task and would quickly confess their need for God's help and guidance. This dependence is good. Many a parent would like to ask the Lord the question Manoah did, *"How shall we order the child and how shall we do unto him?"* (Judges 13:12, KJV). We ask God to *"teach us what we shall do for the child who will be born"* (Judges 13:8).

Thankfully, God has given us this information in the Bible— our manual for raising children. In this lesson we will look at God's instructions for building our precious additions. Decide ahead of time that you will trust His word and follow it as you have those little souls under construction (Prov. 3:5-7). And if you ever find any principle of childrearing in the Bible with which you disagree, just remember that when you take issue with the Bible, you take issue with God!

Our approach in this lesson is simple. We will examine some crucial things we must *do well* as parents from *before* our children are born to the time of adolescence.

MOTIVATION FOR GOOD PARENTING

Why should a parent be motivated to construct the best-built child possible? God's word provides great answers to that question.

- **Because God requires it.** God has placed on parents the responsibility of raising children the way He wants them raised (Eph. 6:4; Col. 3:20-21). An adult who causes a child to sin (and this would include *many* unwitting parents) would be better off eternally wearing a stone collar at the bottom of the sea without an air supply (Matt. 18:5-7)!

- **Because love demands it** (Prov. 3:11-12).

- **Children reflect on their parents.** Parents should desire to avoid the shame and embarrassment involved in receiving the credit (?) for raising an ungodly, rebellious, or shiftless child. A wicked child brings shame and reproach upon his parents (Prov. 28:7; 19:13, 26). Children reflect *on* their parents because they are usually reflections *of* their parents.

- **Children can bring delight or grief to their parents** (Prov. 10:1; 15:20; 23:15-16, 24; 17:21, 25; 19:13; 27:11). Many of your future joys and griefs will be the direct results of the job you do as a parent!

THE GOALS OF PARENTING

The ultimate objective of parenting is to *"train up a child in the way he should go"* so that *"when he is old he will not depart from it"* (Prov. 22:6). The *way* a child should go is *the way of the Lord.* Abraham was to *"command his children and his household after him that they keep the way of the Lord"* (Gen. 18:19).

As we've already mentioned, the task of parents is summed up well in Ephesians 6:4. Children are to be brought up in *"the training and admonition of the Lord."* *Training* here is translated from the Greek word *paideia* which is a word the Greeks used to refer to the broad education and socialization of a child, as well as to the specific instruction, nurture, and discipline needed to arrive at the goal. A Greek child who received training (*paideia*) would be completely steeped in the knowledge and culture of the Greeks. As a result, he would think, talk and act Greek!

Even so, a Christian's child is to be *immersed* in the knowledge of God and the *culture* of Christianity. Vow to give your child to God! Again, this is not something to get serious about some time after they are born. It is a pre-birth decision (1 Sam. 1:11, 26-28).

The *ideal* for every parent is to raise a child who is like Christ. Jesus was the perfect adult and the perfect child. As parents, our duty is to help our children increase *"in wisdom and stature, and in favor with God and man"* just like Jesus did (Luke 2:52). Parents must try to ensure the proper development of their children mentally, physically, spiritually, and socially.

- **Mental Development—Wisdom.** Wisdom is not merely the possession of knowledge, but the discretion to use knowledge correctly—skill. Teaching children the three R's (reading, 'riting, and 'rithmetic) is insufficient; the desire and skill to use that knowledge for good must also be instilled. God's book can give *"the young man knowledge and discretion"* and teach him how to apply it (Prov. 1:4). But children left to their own to "discover" how to use knowledge will be influenced by society, peers, or their own lusts to use it foolishly.

- **Physical Development—Stature.** Parents are to provide the things necessary for a child's proper physical development (1 Tim. 5:8). They must also convey to their children a healthy respect for the body along with the understanding that the true value of a strong and fit body is found in the service it can offer to God (1 Cor. 6:19-20; 1 Tim. 4:8).

- **Spiritual Development—Favor with God.** Children are born on God's "good side" (Matt. 19:14). As they grow, their favor with God should grow as well, and it will if they are taught to do good (Prov. 12:2; 2 Tim. 3:14-17). Many worldly parents are only concerned with the physical, mental, and social development of their children. But for the Christian, our central concern is raising children who will obtain favor from the Lord as adults and in eternity.

Social Development—Favor with men. Jesus interacted well with others while staying true to Himself and His integrity. He certainly had some enemies, but He could count multitudes of people who desired to live right as His friends (Mark 12:37; Luke 7:34; 12:4; John 15:14-15). Parents should strive to instill these same qualities in children. Children need to know how to develop quality friendships with good people (1 Cor. 15:33; Prov. 22:24; 1:10ff.) and how to be quality friends themselves (Prov. 17:17; 18:24). They do not need to be trained to gain social acceptance at all cost. *"Woe unto you when all the world speaks well of you"* (Luke 6:26).

PREPARING FOR PARENTHOOD

As a parent, you should prepare from day one to know your child. They don't come off a "cookie cutter" or an assembly line. Each one is unique.

One concept that may be implied in Proverbs 22:6 is that children come with a certain *bent* or *way* (certain traits, characteristics, talents). This verse encourages us to adapt our training to that *way*. Children are different, and we have to adapt our training efforts accordingly.

How many times have we heard parents say, *"They are so different"*? Pay attention to them. Look closely at each child. It will help you even with their educational training if you can see their *bent*. Those classes they love and in which they do well are clues. Those they hate and don't do so well in are also clues for future vocations. If they take what they love and make it their job, they will never work a day in their life. They have passion for it.

Recognize also that effective discipline may be different for each child; one falls in line with a good, firm word or look, while another will attempt to stand firm against the strongest discipline. You cannot begin effective training until you have taken time to know them.

And get this—the person you will have to work the most on is you. Think about what *you* are to the child. *You are God's agent!* He has delegated His authority to you. If they reject your authority, they are rejecting *God* Himself!

We believe the style of parenting that is Biblical is the same style God uses. *Like Him, you must lead like a shepherd* (Ezek. 34:11-16). You are shepherding a child's heart. Just try to think like a shepherd. A shepherd-parent will do the following:

- Guide his children.

- Help them understand themselves (made by God, for God).

- Lead them to think as the Chief Shepherd thinks.

- Help them understand themselves in relation to the world they live in.

- Help them learn to take a good look at themselves—*what* they did and *why* they did it.

- Lead them to use wisdom and discernment.

- Be willing to do the hard things to save their little lamb.

MAKING A GREAT ENVIRONMENT IN THE HOME

The home has lost twice in our society. At one time, before the industrial revolution, dads worked closer to home, and at times their children could tag along in the fields and workshops. But then, we lost dads to the work world away from the home place. This is understandable and mostly necessary. But then the home lost again when we lost moms to the work world (not always necessary).

Mom is so crucial to the home as a homemaker, a *"keeper at home"* (Titus 2:1-5). This passage depicts a godly woman in charge over her children. Proverbs 31 paints the same picture. If at all possible, we must avoid carting our children off to someone else (particularly daycare), leaving little time for them to be at home with the people that matter the most. The best person to care for your children is you. That's what God calls for *you* to do.

Home needs to be a secure place for kids. Work hard on your relationship as husband and wife so that they do not see constant verbal battles, struggles, and fights. Home must be a *place of love and support.* Encourage them and praise them. Catch them doing right. Spend a lot of time with them. Family nights are great!!

A tremendous bond is built in the early years. Most parents are amazed at how little things are remembered. A friend once said, *"The thing that kept me straight during the teen years was the thought of hurting my dad. We had done so much together, playing baseball in the yard, etc., that I couldn't bear the thought of disappointing him."*

All of this means time at home must be prioritized. We must beware of buzzing here and there and everywhere. Too many extracurricular activities are not good. They can contribute to homes being destroyed while we are busy flitting about from one activity to the next.

THE BEHAVIORS OF PARENTING

Is there some special secret or ability successful parents possess? Are some parents just made to be better than others? We think not. The key behaviors of successful parenting are described in Scripture and can be practiced by any parent who is committed to doing God's will. Sometimes it is said, "They are *so lucky* to have a great family!" Luck had little to do with it. It's like saying, "They are so lucky to live in a clean house." Luck didn't do it. Hard work did.

It is sobering to realize that scientific research seems to indicate that one's own upbringing greatly influences parenting tendencies. Our children will tend to parent their children like we parented them. And that can be either a blessing or a curse. What then are some remaining keys to build our new additions?

LOVE. Parents are obviously to love their children (Titus 2:4). Look at 1 Corinthians 13:4-8 with an eye to how the behaviors of love specifically apply to parenting children. For instance, think about how the fact that love "is kind" might alter the way a loving parent interacts with his child. Love is the basis for all the other parenting behaviors, even punishment (Prov. 13:24).

MODEL. Christians are to serve as good examples before all men (2 Cor. 8:21). This principle applies to the parent-child relationship as much as any other. Parents model behaviors. In large part, children only say what they hear and do what they see. Among the reasons the children of a righteous man are blessed is that they have straight steps to follow, for *"the righteous man walks in his integrity"* (Prov. 20:7). If what they see in us doesn't match what we have taught them, we are in for trouble. Jesus Himself taught against leaders whose walk doesn't match their talk (Mt. 23:3). Through parental example, children should be *shown* the meanings of love, honesty, courage, self-sacrifice, hard work, dedication, forgiveness, and trust.

INSTRUCT. Isaiah 54:13 states, *"All your children shall be taught by the Lord."* When parents use God's book to instruct their children, the children are being instructed *"by the Lord"* (2 Tim. 3:14-17). The instruction parents give children should be filled with Scripture (Deut. 6:6ff; 11:19; Psalm 78:1-6; 2 Tim. 3:15).

Begin from day one teaching them God's word. If you begin reading or singing to them from day one, they will never remember a day when they were not being taught the Bible (2 Tim. 1:5; 3:14-15). Teaching God's word can also be facilitated by the following:

- *A regular time* for teaching of the Bible in your home. Bedtime is wonderful; the kitchen table is good. Pray with them. Teach them to pray.

- *Use of daily life* to teach and share the word (Deut. 6:6-7).

God and godly principles can be easily seen and taught as we move through our day, whether we are sitting, walking by the way, or preparing to lie down for the night.

- ***Choose a local congregation*** that is serious about teaching the children well so that they know the Bible story and how they fit into it.

When we are instructing our children, we must communicate in such a way that they know exactly what we expect and what we will view as disobedience. When possible, as they can grasp it, we should tell them why we are teaching them as we are. Tell them God is your Shepherd too, and He wants you to lead them well. The responsibility of children to heed and obey must be conveyed (Prov.13:1; 15:32, Eph. 6:1; Col. 3:20).

These early years are crucial in training and shaping the direction of the child. If we start early enough, even our pets and service animals can be trained to do tremendous things. Surely our children can be trained too! Like a master painter or sculptor, you must have vision for where you want this thing to go! And remember, the window of time to get the job done is small indeed.

REPROVE, CORRECT, AND PRAISE. When children have done wrong they need to be told so and shown the right way. This is reproof and correction. Proverbs 29:17 promises that if you *"correct your son...he will give you rest."* But don't forget that children not only need to be shown what to do, they also need to be praised for doing it. Letting a child know how pleasing his good behavior is reinforces that behavior. God told Jesus often how pleased He was with Him (Mt. 3:17; 17:5).

DISCIPLINE (PUNISH). Discipline is the entire process: the teaching, the training, the enforcing. Children need to be trained to *be responsible*; chores are needed! Children need to be taught to be *mannerly, to be respectful, to care, and to share*. They need to understand that they are *under authority*. They always will be. As was said a generation ago when the electric chair was a common form of capital punishment, *"You can either learn to respect authority in the high chair, or they will teach you to respect it in the electric chair.*" Some have seen the lack of submission to authority lead to terrible things. It's serious business to God (Rom. 1:30; Col. 3:20-21).

Punishment with the *"rod of correction"* is the God-given means for chastening a disobedient child (Prov. 22:15). Proverbs 13:24 teaches that such loving discipline should be swift and appropriate: "*He who spares his rod hates his son, but he who loves him disciplines him promptly.*" The goal is to improve the child while there is still hope to do so (Prov. 19:18; 23:13-14).

The *"Terrible Two's"* (or somewhere there about) is a time to get this issue of who is in charge settled and burned into their mind. True obedience involves three things: *without challenge, without excuse, without delay.* When you have spoken for the first time, you have spoken for the last time.

It is essential to know that the rod *and* reproof are needed (Prov. 22:15; 29:15, 17; 23:13-19, 22, 26). *Talking* to the child along with the rod is a must. Don't just jerk them up and spank them with very little teaching. Take time if possible to seek a private place to do your job well. Be under control when you administer discipline.

This is not to say that other punishments can't be used (privileges taken away, etc.). They can be very effective but the rod must remain as an often *needed* tool. Hug them afterward and remind them of why you must punish them and how much you love them.

We cannot emphasize enough that whenever there is a contest of the wills, the parent must win!! If a child ever learns that he or she can beat you or manipulate you, you are in for a lot of heartache. They can learn very early. If a round of discipline does not sweeten the disposition, go back for more. Our heavenly Father does not give up on disciplining us (Heb. 12:5-11)! You must not take the easy route at this age. You must do the hard work. If you don't, you will pay a heavy price later!!

The most beautiful part of this is that children understand discipline often better than some adults do. Don't stop too soon with spankings. I talked to a woman once who got her last one at sixteen. Judgment will be needed. At later ages, other punishments may be necessary and more effective, but don't stop too soon.

BE CONSISTENT. It is important to be consistent in all aspects of parenting, but especially in the area of discipline. Couples who do not agree about discipline, or parents who individually are inconsistent in applying it, frustrate and anger children. This is sinful (Col. 3:21). As head of the family, the *father* is given *primary* responsibility for seeing that the children are raised in the training and admonition of the Lord. Fathers should take the lead in this area to insure that discipline is consistent and fair.

- *Say what you mean. Mean what you say. If discipline is promised, you must follow through.* Sometimes it will not be convenient and will take you away from something you were doing or wanting to do. But don't let it slide.

- *Make sure that your walk matches your talk.*

- *Have fences and guidelines that don't move, and give security to a child.* The angriest kids today never had parents who cared enough to put up fences. They wish they had.

- *Be consistent in church attendance.* Make sure the kids see that it comes first. "Are we going to worship services?" is a question that should never be asked. The entire family should *know* that if it is possible to go, every member of the family *will* go! Make arrangements with coaches, band directors, scout leaders, etc., when there are conflicts. Have an understanding upfront that honoring God in worship is the number one priority.

Perhaps more could be said, but this much we know; if these

things are *not done* in these years, get ready for the roughest of rides in the adolescent years and perhaps for the rest of your life. *Do them* and you will smile many times over; your heart will be able to rest, and your children will one day return and say, *"Thank you"* (Proverbs 31:28). They will implement the same in the rearing of your grandchildren. Did somebody say "legacy"? *"You, and your son, and your grandson"* (Dt. 6:2).

PRAY. We began this lesson by noting that many parents feel challenged beyond their abilities with the responsibilities of parenting. We need God's aid. We need God's wisdom. And we can have it, if we are willing to pray for it (James 1:5). Someone has said, "When all else fails, pray." It would be much better if parents would begin praying long before all else fails.

QUESTIONS:

1. Why can children be a source of both great joy and great concern to parents?

2. Give some scriptural motivations for parents to do their jobs well. Which do you think is the strongest motivation?

3. From a biblical perspective, what are the goals of parenting?

4. Would you agree that Jesus must have been the perfect child?

   In what four areas did the boy Jesus increase, according to Luke 2:52?

5. Why is it important for parents to know their child?

   Can you think of ways parents can help children know themselves?

6. What are some keys to making the home environment conducive to bringing children up God's way?

7. Read over the behaviors of love found in 1 Corinthians 13:4-8 and be ready to discuss how these behaviors of love apply to parenting.

8. Do parents have a God-given responsibility to be good examples to their children? What Bible passages teach this?

9. Does the primary responsibility for teaching God's word to children lie with the church, the preacher, or the parents? Defend your answer from scripture.

10. Does the Bible encourage parents to discipline their children by spanking them? According to scripture, what are the consequences of doing this or leaving it undone?

11. What problems are caused when a parent is not consistent in teaching, modeling, or disciplining a child according to God's word?

   Are the same problems likely to occur when two parents do not agree on these things? Explain.

12. What place does prayer have in raising a child? What should parents pray for and about?

Chapter 13

Managing Money

There is an oft told story about a little boy who worked for days creating a toy boat. When he took the boat down to the sea for the first time, its sails caught a strong breeze, and the boat drifted away. The little boy stood there with tears streaming down his face as he watched his toy boat, the one he had worked on for so long, drift off the horizon and out of sight.

Some weeks later, the little boy was in the city and was walking by a pawn shop. In the window he saw his toy boat. He ran through the door of the shop, up to the owner, and cried, "Sir you have my boat in the window. It was a boat I made myself."

The pawnbroker replied, "Son, it may have been your boat at one time, but it is mine now. If you want your boat back, you will have to do as all my customers do and buy it."

Over the next few weeks the little boy did odd jobs around the neighborhood; he mowed grass, carried out garbage, walked dogs, washed cars, and painted fences until he had enough money to buy his boat back. He then went down to the pawnbroker and purchased his toy boat. As he walked away from the store, holding the boat tightly, he was heard to say, "Little boat: I made you...I lost you...I found you...I bought you...and now you are mine, all mine."

Those words are the words God must speak to us. He created us. He lost us in sin. He found us through the cross. And He bought us with the blood of His Son. Now, we belong to Him—lock, stock and barrel! And the implications of God's purchase of us touches every aspect of our lives, our homes, and our families.

We live in a country where people love to talk about what is "mine." It begins early in life as children fight over what's "mine." One father was trying to teach this very early to his daughter. One day she asked, "Are these chairs God's? He can't have *my* high chair." See? They start early with their concept of private ownership. At bedtime, the little girl put on her long pajama shirt, which she called her "shommy shirt," and asked, "Is this God's shommy shirt? Did He wear it when He was little?" Well, at least she was catching on to some degree.

Over the next little while try to listen to yourself and see how often you say something is "mine." Yet, the Bible blows to bits the mindset that is stuck on "I, me, mine, myself." It destroys all arrogance and belief of purely private ownership and teaches us that even our money belongs to Him and our finances come under His control. But there is freedom in being bought by God and running our finances according to His guidelines and principles.

D-I-V-O-R-C-E BECAUSE OF M-O-N-E-Y

One of the greatest causes for divorce is financial stress. Counselors see the problem often in their offices. A national survey revealed that 64 percent of married couples frequently argue about spending habits. Statistics suggest that as many as 80% of couples who split up say that a major cause was money problems. There is a great need to see what the Bible has to say about money and the use of it, so that our homes can have financial peace.

Before we begin our study of scriptural principles for managing money, let's clear up a couple of common misconceptions about money.

First, having more money will almost certainly NOT resolve your financial stress. The majority of people in the economic middle class mistakenly believe that if they could earn an extra one or two hundred dollars a month, they could make it financially. The truth is that most money problems will not be solved by larger incomes. People spend according to what they make, so making more often only enlarges money issues. Solomon said, *"When goods increase, they increase who eat them"* (Eccl. 5:11).

The second misconception is that money is inherently evil. In and of itself, money is morally neutral. Take some money out of your pocket and lay it on a table. What harm can it do? None. It lies there doing nothing. But our attitude toward it and our use of it does cause problems and can say a lot about us (Luke 16:10-11; 21:1-4). In many ways, your attitude toward money is a barometer of your spiritual life. The man who struggles to be disciplined with his money often struggles with spiritual disciplines as well. Think about how often Jesus used money in connection with spiritual things. It is also a good predictor of your ability to maintain positive relationships with your fellow human beings—including your family.

KEEPING MONEY IN PROPER PERSPECTIVE

When our concept of the true nature of material wealth is inaccurate, our attitudes about it will be inappropriate. As already stated, a healthy view of money begins with realizing that all our money and material blessings come from God (Psa. 50:10-12; 1 Chr. 29:11-12; James 1:17). It belongs to Him, and He disposes of it as He wishes (1 Sam. 2:7-8). It is also God who gives us the power to gain money and enjoy its benefits (Deut. 8:18; Eccl. 5:19).

A steward is a manager of what belongs to another (1 Cor. 4:1-2; Luke 16:1-2). That is what we are. God has given us our resources as stewards and expects us to use them wisely according to His guidelines. Knowing they are His, and that He has the right to give or take away as He sees fit, relieves us of a lot of stress.

John Wesley once said as his house was burning down, *"The Lord's house burned down. One less responsibility for me."* So, if you lost something, you really didn't, because you never owned it to begin with. Understanding that the Lord may do with His possessions as He pleases is an extremely helpful and calming realization. Job knew this (Job 1:21).

"Affluenza" is an epidemic sweeping the country. We have to be careful not to be swept away in our desire for more and more (Luke 12:16-21). We are warned about loving money (1 Tim. 6:10). A wonderful attitude toward material things is found in Proverbs 30:8-9. Riches and poverty both have their temptations and snares, and so *the wise man* desires neither. How much better we all would be if we had the wise man's spirit. It has been called the "middle way." We must learn to love simplicity and be content (1 Tim. 6:6-10).

WHAT TO DO AS MONEY COMES IN

Jesus said that *"one's life does not consist in the abundance of the things he possesses"* (Luke 12:15). Understanding that truth will have a tremendous impact on your family life. Your life is not made of money; it is made of relationships. People matter far more than money. No man on his death bed says, "I wish I had spent more time at the office."

Money is to be managed and used as a tool to enhance relationships rather than misused and allowed to control and ruin relationships. We can make friends with what Jesus called "unrighteous mammon," and it could be that our kindness to those friends results in them seeking to know more about the God who made us so generous and caring. If they become Christians, they may on that Great Day welcome you into the eternal home (Luke 16:9). Wouldn't that be a rewarding use of the money in our own pockets?

Biblically speaking, good money management involves paying close attention to three areas of financial responsibility— ***giving, providing, and saving.***

GIVING. Giving should be our first priority when it comes to managing our money. Scriptural giving is focused on honoring God with our possessions, either by giving directly back to Him or by passing a portion of our blessings on to others. Honoring the Lord with our wealth must be a priority (Prov. 3:9-10)! Failing to give God that which honors Him is like robbing Him (Mal. 3:8-12)!

Giving will seldom hurt the bottom line financially. As the previous verses indicated, people who give more tend to receive more—a truth that is also born out in Proverbs 11:24-25, Ecclesiastes 11:1, Luke 6:38, and 2 Corinthians 9:6-11. And even if this seems not to be the case in the short term, the attitude of a liberal giver toward material things is such that he or she will feel more blessed even with less (Acts 20:35). One of the greatest blessings of living simply is having something to give to others in need. This spirit of generosity is a great source of happiness (Eph. 4:28; Acts 20:35).

PROVIDING. Even people who are not particularly religious understand that working to provide for one's self and family is right and honorable. No wonder the apostle Paul says that *"if anyone does not provide for his own, and especially for those of his household, he has denied the faith and is **worse than** an unbeliever"* (1 Tim. 5:8).

Note the focus on working for a living in 2 Thessalonians 3:6-14. Paul commands, *"If anyone will not work, neither shall he eat"* (3:10), and that people are to *"work in quietness and eat their own bread"* (3:12). From this passage we can see that God demands that His children perform honorable work to provide for themselves. This responsibility is so serious that a Christian who does not do it cannot be considered faithful to the Lord.

SAVING. Saving is a confusing topic for many Christians. Many seem to think that saving for the future implies a lack of trust in God to take care of us, and in some cases it does. Anytime we trust in our money and material possessions more than in God, we are in error, just like the rich fool that Jesus describes in Luke 12:16-21. We must put God first and trust that He will take care of us now and in the future (Matt. 6:33).

However, this does not mean that God wants us to abandon wisdom when it comes to managing money and saving for the future. In Proverbs 21:20, the Bible says that, *"There is desirable treasure, and oil in the dwelling of the wise, but a foolish man squanders it."* The translation of this verse in the *Contemporary English Version* makes the point even clearer: *"Be sensible and store up precious treasures; don't waste them like a fool."*

The Scriptures not only encourage careful saving; they also warn us not to ruin our financial futures by taking on obligations that we are not able to pay back (Prov. 22:7, 26-27).

One of the soundest financial principles is simply to ***spend less than you make!*** Do not be careless. Do some financial planning (Prov. 27:23-24). Where are you? Where will you be years from now? It will be a great blessing to be able to pass on something to your children (Prov. 13:22). Get all the use you can out of the big ticket items before you rush out for another (car, refrigerator, etc.). A car is good if it takes you where you need to go much like a garbage can is good if it gets garbage to the street. Our cars must not be viewed as status symbols, but as tools to transport us safely and efficiently. Count the cost of all financial decisions (Luke 14:28-30). Be careful about cosigning (Prov. 17:18).

NEVER FORGET WHERE THE TRUE RICHES ARE

If you are God's child, you are already rich and possess all things! *"There is one who makes himself rich, yet has nothing; And one who makes himself poor, yet has great riches"* (Prov. 13:7; see also Matt. 6:19-21; Rev. 2:9; 2 Cor. 8:9; 1 Cor. 3:21-23; Col. 2:2).

Somebody once said, *"We must quit spending money to buy things we don't need to impress people we don't like."* Do not let money become your master. Make it your slave. Realize that God must be number one in your life (Matt. 6:24)! Make your money serve you, setting you free to serve and glorify God. Following these God-given principles will bless your life abundantly. By God's grace, you will go through life with greater ease and less stress.

QUESTIONS:

1. What role do financial problems play in troubled marriages and divorce? What are the underlying attitudes towards money that will cause it to become a problem in a marriage?

2. From whom do all material blessings come? Who gives us the ability to make money and enjoy its benefits?

3. How will seeing ourselves as stewards of our possessions help us keep the right attitude toward money and material things?

4. Do you agree that "affluenza" is an epidemic sweeping our country? Give some concrete examples of affluenza.

5. What metaphors or symbolic comparisons are used in the following verses to illustrate that people who give more tend to receive more?

    - Proverbs 11:24-25
    - Ecclesiastes 11:1
    - Luke 6:38
    - 2 Corinthians 9:6-11

6. We can do three things with our money—save it, spend it, or give it. Each of these is necessary, but they all must be kept in proper balance. In relationships, it is important to agree on what that balance is. That agreement starts with understanding how each person feels about what is being done with the money. This exercise is a step toward achieving that understanding. Complete the following, answering honestly:

- Saving money makes me feel _____

- I would like to save _____ (more or less) money.

- The main reasons to save money are _____
  _____

- Spending money makes me feel _____.

- I would like to spend _____ (more or less) money.

- Giving money makes me feel _____.

- I would like to give _____ (more or less) money.

- To which organizations or individuals would I like to give money? Why?

What do your answers indicate about your own attitude toward money?

In what way do you need to improve your attitude?

7. In 2 Thessalonians 3:6-14, Paul gives at least two privileges that should be taken away from a man who refuses to work to support himself. What are they?

8. Read 1 Timothy 6:17-19, Matthew 6:19-20, and Luke 16:9. From these verses, what is the BEST use of your money?

Chapter 14

Prayer Power
Keeping God in Charge of Construction

When we began this study and broke ground for our dream homes, we made sure that it was clear that our construction was doomed for failure without the Lord as our Architect/Contractor and the Bible as our blueprint. *"Unless the Lord builds the house, they labor in vain who build it"* (Psalm 127:1).

To accomplish the enormous task of building a home that will help our families heavenward, we absolutely must **undergird the whole project with prayer**. Like Nehemiah of old, who got on his knees and prayed his way through one of the greatest building projects ever accomplished, husbands and fathers must be leaders from the knees up!

But tragically, although they know better, too many married Christians seldom refer to God's word for specific guidance in marriage and rarely seek His help for their families in prayer. As a result, their marriages are not really that much different from marriages of those in the world; God is not in charge!

TWO-WAY COMMUNICATION

As we studied in an earlier lesson, communication is at the heart of every good relationship. We come to know others by communicating with them, and we use that knowledge to bond with them. If the knowledge isn't accurate or good, the bond won't be either.

Good communication with God is essential not only to your relationship with Him, but also to your relationships with others. Can you imagine what a home might end up looking like if you never talked to your contractor? Likewise, listening to God's instructions for family relationships and asking Him for guidance in those relationships will enable us to build dream homes!

Good communication is two-way communication. Ever tried to keep conversation going with someone who wouldn't talk? How frustrating! You don't have that burden with God. He is a talker, and He loves to talk with You. Please understand that the conversation isn't just for you. The Lord actually enjoys being with you too as you meet to talk. God TALKS TO YOU when you read the Bible, His word. We TALK TO HIM when we pray. Not meeting with Him is to rob yourself, but you also rob Him of the fellowship He wanted with you.

Two-way communication is responsive. Our guess is that most folks read their Bible and pray as two distinct activities— doing one and at some point doing the other. But have you ever considered doing both at the same time, combining them to make a dialogue between yourself and God? This is so powerful, and it is more like an ordinary conversation. You first let God speak as you read a passage, and then you respond. Let God speak again by moving to the next passage. Then, you respond again. See how simple that is? And the best part is He will talk as long as you like.

Think about it. We expect God to respond to our prayers (Psa. 119:26). But why expect Him to do all the responding? We should respond to His words as well (Prov. 28:9). So, when you read the Bible, talk to God about the things that He is telling you in His word. Choose to read often the scriptures that address godly character, Christlikeness, fatherhood, motherhood, and other home-related themes. Become comfortable as godly fathers and mothers doing these things:

- Ask God a question.

  - *Does this apply to me? If so, how?*
  - *Does this mean what I think it means?*
  - *How is this related to other Scripture?*

- Ask Him for help in understanding (Psa. 119:34, 169, 27).

- Praise God for His wisdom, power, justice, comfort, love, mercy, or grace as seen in the passage (Psa. 119:7, 76, 164).

- Thank God for things He shares that bring His light to a subject or bring comfort (Psa. 119:62).

- Ask God to help you apply what you have learned by giving you the necessary strength or wisdom to do so (Psa. 119:9-10, 16-17, 32, 133, 173).

Talking with God should be a daily part of every Christian's life. It is a surefire way to keep your dream home project on the right track. Your roles, attitudes, and interactions will be God-honoring and a great example. We strongly recommend starting your day by meeting with God. The first activity of the day tends to rule the day. It is not always easy to rise out of bed, but you simply must exercise "mind over mattress." Successful homebuilders don't like rising early any more than others do. But remember: "Successful people have a habit of doing the things others don't like to do." If another time of day works better for you, that's fine—but just be sure to find your closet (room) and talk to your Father (Matt. 6:6).

APPLYING PRAYER POWER

Prayer is the single most powerful resource available to the Christian. It is not that prayer by itself is powerful. Prayer brings power into our homes because **the One to whom we pray is all-powerful**! Having electrical power coming to our homes is of no benefit unless we "plug in" or "flip the switch." Likewise, through prayer we tap into the boundless power of our Almighty Father who can do more to help us than we can even imagine (Eph. 3:20).

Prayer can help in every human relationship. The apostle Paul commands that *"supplications, prayers, intercessions, and giving of thanks be made for all men"* (1 Tim. 2:1). Yet prayer often remains an untapped resource in the marriage relationship. Why do you think it is that husbands and wives may not pray for one another as they should? Could it be that we lack faith in God's power or somehow believe that He is not interested in the well-being of our families?

Two forms of prayer mentioned by Paul in 1 Timothy 2:1 are especially useful in crafting strong families: *intercession* and *giving of thanks.* Let's delve into these forms of prayer and learn how to apply them to benefit our most important relationships.

INTERCESSION

Intercession involves going to God on behalf of another. Pleading for the well-being of another immediately invests us fully in their welfare. This is what loving one another is all about. The Lord wants us to be as committed to the welfare of others as He is. The Lord wants us to battle for those we love just as He has battled for us. And just as PVC pipe is needed to channel water to different rooms in the house, intercession opens a pipeline from God to the ones we care about the most.

Satan is surely warring to pull down your home. Don't let him use you to do it. Sometimes we do war all wrong. Should you ever have conflict with a spouse or child...**fight for them** rather than wasting so much time fighting *with* them. They are not the enemy. They are victims of the enemy. Your fight is not with them. Your fight is with the devil and his forces who may be currently ensnaring them (Eph. 6:10).

Do war the right way by praying for God to work in their lives to turn them around. Ask Him to change your spirit toward them, to give you patience, and to help you gain the victory through gentleness and longsuffering. You need God warring with you. Fight in His strength alone. Yours will fail (Eph. 6:10).

We need to have Samuel's understanding of the importance of such intercessory prayer. He said to Israel, *"Far be it from me that I should sin against the LORD in ceasing to pray for you"* (1 Sam. 12:23). Could it be that it is *actually a sin* not to pray for someone when you know that God wants you to pray for them? (James 4:17).

Some great examples of intercessory prayer are found in Scripture:

- Abraham pleading with God not to destroy the righteous with Sodom and Gomorrah (Gen. 18:16-33).

- Moses begging God not to wipe out Israel after the incident with the golden calf (Exo. 32:7-14).

- Jesus praying for the protection and sanctification of His apostles (John 17:6-19).

In each of these examples, notice how the one offering the intercession bases his request on the premise that it will bring glory to God the Father! This principle should be applied to prayers we offer for our spouses and our children. Make a connection in your prayer between what you are asking God to do for your loved one and how it will help your loved one glorify God. If no connection can be made, it's probably not a prayer that should be prayed! If God can't be glorified in it, the thing you are asking for cannot be something that a Christian should want (1 Cor. 10:31).

GIVING THANKS

Giving thanks to God for the person for whom we are praying helps us pray more effectively; it clarifies for us the reasons that person is special to us and conveys those reasons to God. The apostle Paul often coupled thanksgiving and intercession in his prayers for others. Note how Paul's thanksgiving is tied to his intercessory prayer in Romans 1:8-10, 1 Corinthians 1:4-8, Philippians 1:3-6, 2 Timothy 1:3-5, and Philemon 4-5.

PRAYERS FOR CARES

The Lord taught that we would have cares. Consider the Lord's teaching in the parable of the sower. See how He mentions our cares (Luke 8:4-8, 11-15). There are some cares that we have daily that are not wrong, but they become wrong when we allow them to choke God out of our lives. Our chief care must always be the Lord and His work, and we should make sure that other cares do not choke Him out (1 Cor. 7:34-35).

The devil's desire is to turn our cares into fears—to cause us to worry and fret and have little faith and trust. Jesus addresses the problem of worry in Matthew 6:25-34. He teaches us that worry accomplishes nothing!

Some refuse to accept the Lord's teachings on the folly of worry. One confused individual once said, *"Don't tell me it doesn't help to worry. Most of the things I worry about never happen!"* The truth— *"Worry is like a rocking chair. It gets you moving but you don't go anywhere."* If our number one priority is the kingdom of God and His righteousness, what is there to worry about? The Lord is with us in our most important concern!

Another great passage on this subject is Philippians 4:6-7. Let's make certain to get out of this passage everything that's in it!

- What are we to be anxious for? *Nothing!*

- What should we do with our anxieties? *Turn them over to God!*

- If we truly trust God and give Him our anxieties, what will come from Him? *Peace!*

- What will be guarded by God? *Our hearts and minds!*

The opposite of *worry* is *trust.* Worry is an indicator that we have work to do when it comes to our trust in God to work in our lives for good. I believe a story in the Old Testament is a classic on dealing with worry. It's the story of King Jehoshaphat as he faced a tremendous enemy (2 Chron. 20). Jehoshaphat overcame his fears through prayer. He told God what we will also have to tell Him at times. He admitted having no power of his own and added, *"nor do we know what to do. But our eyes are upon You"* (20:12). In verse 15, he declares that the battle belongs to God! God gave incredible victory without an arrow being fired. They sang their way to victory!

What faith! Instead of fretting in a time of worry or trouble, we must commit the battle to God! We must always look to God, not circumstances (Matt. 14:22-33). God can be trusted to take even bad things and make them work for the good of those who love Him (Rom. 8:28).

Trust the Lord at every turn in your home life. Follow His instructions. Seek His guidance. He can take a crumbling home and turn it into your dream home. *"He is able even to subdue all things to Himself"* (Phil. 3:21). His infinite power is matched by His unfailing love. He only wants the best for you and your family. Let Him have His way, and He will make your life, your home, and your eternity more beautiful than you could ever imagine. This is our prayer for you and for ourselves as we build according to the plans of the Great Architect!

QUESTIONS:

1. What metaphors are used in the following verses to
    describe how those in a close relationship with God will
    feel about receiving His words?

    - Jeremiah 15:16
    - Psalm 119:103
    - 1 Peter 2:2

2. How did the Psalmist respond to God's word in Psalm
    119:12-16?

3. What requests does the Psalmist make to God in Psalm
    119:33-40 that relate to helping the Psalmist learn and
    apply God's word in his life?

4. What guidelines for intercessory prayer can be gleaned
    from the following passages?

    - How important is it that we actually ask (Matt. 7:7-8)?

    - How important is it that we ask unselfishly (James
      4:2-3)?

    - How important is it that we ask according to God's
      will (1 John 5:14-15)?

    - How important is it that we ask with a clean
      conscience (1 John 3:21-22)?

5. In 1 Peter 3:7, husbands are told to do certain things with respect to their wives so that *"your prayers may not be hindered."*

    - What are some things implied in 1 Peter 3:7, or from your personal experience, that would hinder one partner's prayers for the other?

    - What are some of the keys to effective prayer found in 1 Peter 3:8-12?

6. Have you ever "warred" in the wrong way in your family? What adverse effects did it have on those you wanted to change? What is the right way to war?

7. Listed below are nine principles for effective prayer gleaned from 1 Peter 3:8-11. They have been worded as "I" statements to enable you to rate yourself from 0-10. Ten means that the statement describes you all the time, and zero means that it describes you none of the time.

    _____ I seek to understand feelings and thoughts of other family members.
    _____ I want to be of one mind with my family.
    _____ I have compassion and sympathy for each member of my family when he or she talks to me about a problem.
    _____ I normally put my family's interests above my own.
    _____ I treat my family with courtesy and respect in public and private.

_____ I do not return "insult for insult" when someone in my family does or says something that hurts me.

_____ I say something positive to bless a family member when he or she hurts or wrongs me.

_____ I do not deceive my family.

_____ I seek peace with my family.

8. What are the keys to using prayer to rid us of care? (In answering, give thought to how priorities, specific prayer requests, and trust figure into prayers for cares.)

ABOUT THE AUTHORS

Steve Klein and Jeff May are Christians who live in Limestone County, Alabama, and who preach God's word wherever and whenever they have opportunity. They enjoy loving their families, appreciating God's creation, working as servants of God, and anticipating the glories of heaven.

They are the co-authors of *Heaven: O For A Home With God* which is available from AHomewithGod.com, Amazon.com, or select religious bookstores.

Jeff is also the author of *Hoof Prints to HIS Prints,* a devotional book designed for hunters and non-hunters alike who are searching for meaning in life. It is available from woods2word.com, Amazon.com, or select religious bookstores.

CPSIA information can be obtained
at www.ICGtesting.com
Printed in the USA
LVHW081317250321
682469LV00029B/520